FRANKENSTEIN

PENETRATING THE SECRETS OF NATURE

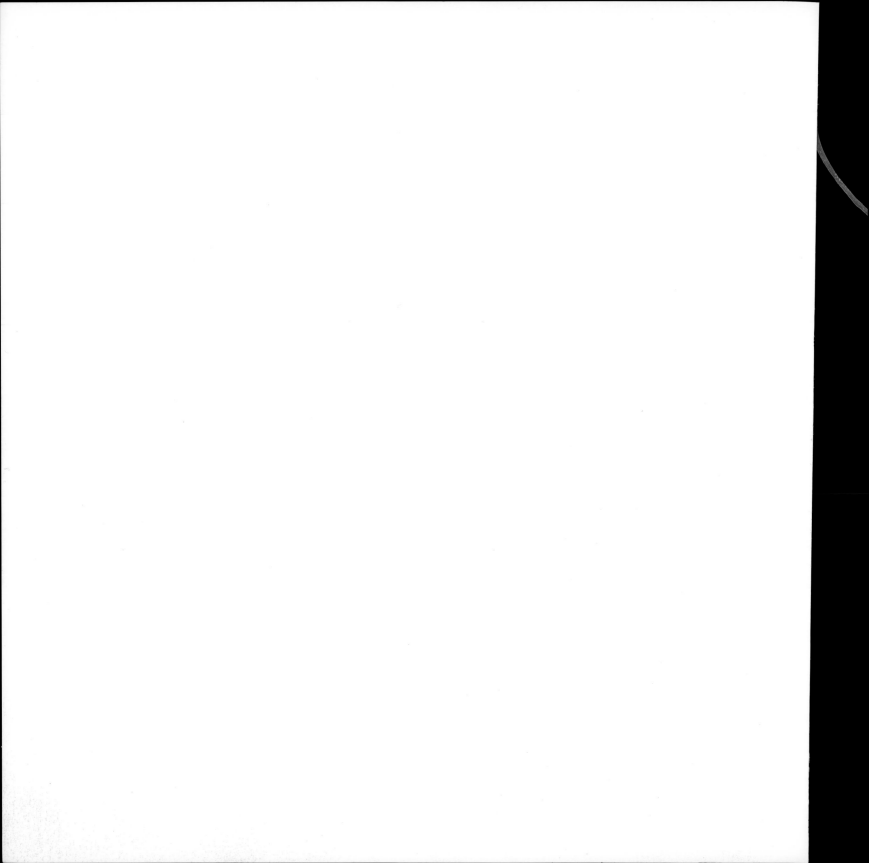

FRANKENSTEIN

PENETRATING THE SECRETS OF NATURE

An Exhibition by the National Library of Medicine

Visiting Curator: Susan E. Lederer

Exhibition Director: Elizabeth Fee

Head, Exhibition Program: Patricia Tuohy

Rutgers University Press
New Brunswick, New Jersey, and London

Library of Congress Cataloguing in Publication
Data and British Library Cataloguing in Publication
Data is available upon request.

Manufactured in China

Published in conjunction with the exhibition Frankenstein: Penetrating the Secrets of Nature organized by the
History of Medicine Division, National Library of Medicine.
Exhibition Director: Elizabeth Fee
Head, Exhibition Program: Patricia Tuohy

Catalogue Design: Troy Hill
Cover photograph: Courtesy Ronald V. Borst/Hollywood Movie Posters
Reproduced courtesy Universal Studios Licensing, Inc.

CONTENTS

DIRECTOR'S INTRODUCTION

Donald A.B. Lindberg, M.D.
Director, National Library of Medicine

My interest in the Frankenstein show stemmed quite directly from viewing David Rees's exhibition of a mannequin of the Frankenstein monster and an imaginative set of spark generators at the Bakken Museum of Electricity and Life in Minneapolis, Minnesota. True to the theme of this fascinating museum, founded by a major manufacturer of cardiac pacemakers, the Frankenstein part of the museum centered on the electrification that our childhood movie experiences taught us could, if not actually bring life to "things," at least cause the muscles and limbs to jump about. Actually David's mannequin, modeled after the 1931 movie *Frankenstein*, resembled an "electric chair" apparatus for ending life as much as it did an imaginable source of life creation.

Even more interesting were the potential connections to mathematical models of muscle innervation, Einthoven's recordings of the EKG signals of the human heart, and the mysteries of reflexes, human brain cell signaling, and memory—all in their way electrical phenomena.

In any event, I was hooked. His was a captivating idea, and it seemed that the National Library of Medicine should have a Frankenstein exhibition.

When I passed along these ideas, Elizabeth Fee was immediately enthusiastic and supportive. I hasten to note, however, that the talented group of historians, planners, and interpreters that she brought together have gone far beyond anything I imagined, both in the implications of the intellectual ideas inherent in the Frankenstein book, but also in explaining the actions and relations of the historical persons that made up the spicy world of Mary Shelley and her circle.

Here I must warn the reader. The person who enters Mary Shelley land will not be frighted with goblins and nightmares. On the contrary, the reader will suddenly be immersed in the amazing population of teenage—but decidedly sophisticated—Mary Shelley and her circle.

Putting behind us the great literary and scientific figures who adorned Mary's childhood and womanhood, we moderns at the National Library of Medicine took to the movies. The Library sponsored a fascinating series of "Thursday Nights at the Movies" in the auditorium of the Lister Hill Center. Here an historical program of Frankenstein movies—and preceding lectures—was offered to "the public." And the public came! Old and young movie buffs slightly outnumbered medical historians, but the theater was often full, and all had a very good time. For me, re-seeing *Young Frankenstein* after the predecessor series of Thomas Edison's *Frankenstein* and the classic Boris Karloff *Frankenstein* was an amazing experience! The already outrageously funny Wilder lines now could be understood in the fullness of their parody of the directorial styles of the earlier movies—as well as the earlier cinematic interpretations of the Shelley novel.

Not to be outdone by stagecraft, life stepped in in 1997. Suddenly scientists at the National Institutes of Health were brought face to face with the ideas and characters and threats and fears of Mary Shelley's times. The cloning of Dolly the sheep took center stage. The newspapers and magazines reminded us in a moment that all the old fears of transplanting animal parts (and spirits?), of going beyond what was proper, and of "playing God" were once again very much in question. Who should live? Who should die? How hard should one try to save life? Should one transplant organs? Animal organs? How obtained? Amazingly we found the White House and the National Institutes of Health director obliged to make public statements on the age-old "Frankenstein" questions!

So—dear reader—please enjoy this grand catalogue and the show. Please enter the stage of the nineteenth century's most liberated and most vulnerable woman, Mary Godwin Shelley.

PROLOGUE

Elizabeth Fee, Ph.D.
Chief, History of Medicine Division
National Library of Medicine

For nearly two hundred years, the story of Frankenstein has gripped our imaginations. *Frankenstein: Penetrating the Secrets of Nature* is an exhibition about the history of science and medicine and also about the contemporary questions that engage all of us: public minded citizens, policy makers, scientists, and ethicists. Issues of cloning and genetic engineering raise questions about the human implications of scientific and technological advances that are troubling to many. "Frankenstein," as myth and as metaphor, can be helpful in crystallizing and helping us to examine these fears.

This exhibition involves literature and ethics as well as science and history. It examines Mary Shelley's remarkable life and the evolution of her classic novel, *Frankenstein*, in literature and popular culture since its publication in 1818. We see how the monster in *Frankenstein* has been transformed during the last two centuries from an articulate creature who is curious about the world and seeks human relationships, to the speechless murderer of later plays and films such as the 1931 *Frankenstein* starring Boris Karloff. Just as Mary Shelley drew upon the science of her time to craft her story, so too did the filmmakers of the 1930s draw upon the fears and anxieties of their historical period, brilliantly reflecting them in their radical reinterpretation. Today, images of Boris Karloff playing Frankenstein's monster are indelibly imprinted on our minds—so much so, that few of us may remember Mary Shelley's original novel.

When we decided to create a Frankenstein exhibition, we invited Susan Lederer to be our visiting curator. A fine historian, Dr. Lederer is the author of *Subjected to Science: Human Experimentation in America before the Second World War* and she is widely known for her work on ethics. She also has a nice sense of playfulness. When I asked Sue if she would be curator for our show, she said, "Yes, as long as we can do body parts." Of course, I agreed. The resulting exhibition was largely the work of Sue Lederer but also of Patricia Tuohy and her very talented exhibition staff.

The original exhibition at the National Library of Medicine caused great interest and some puzzled inquiries. Why would the National Institutes of Health mount a major exhibition on *Frankenstein*? Our mission at the Library is to make the latest and most accurate scientific information about health and disease readily available to the widest possible public; we felt that by addressing head-on the public's fears about xenotransplantation, cloning, and genetic engineering, and by encouraging people to take maximum benefit from our many resources of information about health and medicine, we could simultaneously educate and inform, while creating an exhibition that would present difficult scientific issues in a manner engaging to children, their parents, and the many scientific and medical visitors to the Library. We were delighted by the enthusiastic reception, and even more delighted that the American Library Association is now sending a traveling version of the exhibition to eighty carefully selected libraries across the country.

Frankenstein lives! We hope you enjoy the encounter.

Untitled, 1991
Mitsuaki Iwago (b. 1950)
Courtesy Mitsuaki Iwago/Minden Pictures

FRANKENSTEIN
PENETRATING THE SECRETS OF NATURE

Susan E. Lederer, Ph.D.

For nearly two hundred years, *Frankenstein*, the tale of a young man of science who creates a monstrosity by animating dead human flesh, has gripped our imaginations and haunted our nightmares. Mary Shelley was only twenty years old when the first edition of her novel *Frankenstein; or, The Modern Prometheus* appeared in London in 1818. Ever since that time, Shelley's conception of both the young scientist and his creature have endured in Western culture. Today many people know the Frankenstein monster from film and television rather than the novel, yet there are striking differences between Mary Shelley's *Frankenstein* and the twentieth-century myth of scientific ambition and destruction. The first part of this exhibition highlights Mary Shelley's novel and the context in which she conceived the original *Frankenstein*. In Shelley's telling, the creature begins as a rational being, who, abandoned by his maker, undertakes both a process of self-education and a search for human companionship. The monster's descent into murder and mayhem results from his rage at his creator, his alienation from other human beings, and the continued ill-treatment he receives from the people he encounters.

In the early twentieth century, Shelley's original monster underwent a radical transformation at the hands of Hollywood filmmakers, who adapted the story for mass audiences. The second part of the exhibition focuses on the redefinition of the Frankenstein myth in popular culture. In the Hollywood tale, the fate of the Frankenstein monster becomes a moral lesson illustrating the punishment for ambitious scientists who seek to usurp the place of God by creating life. More than a moral lesson, the celluloid Frankenstein story is a powerful metaphor for addressing the ways in which American society responds to the rapid pace of discoveries in biology and medicine, discoveries that challenge traditional understandings of what it means to be human. The third section of the exhibition examines the continuing power of the Frankenstein story to articulate concerns raised by new developments in biomedicine such as cloning and xenografting (the use of animal organs in human bodies), and the role responsible scientists and citizens play in the ongoing dialogue to determine the acceptable limits of scientific and medical advances.

Mary Shelley
Reginald Easton (d. 1893)
Courtesy The Bodleian Library, University of
Oxford, Shelley relics (d)

Mary Shelley was just eighteen years old and
the unmarried mother of two children when
she experienced her "waking dream" about a
pale student and the monster he creates, a
dream that would become her first novel,
Frankenstein.

THE BIRTH OF FRANKENSTEIN

Frankenstein; or, The Modern Prometheus, first took shape during the "wet, uncongenial summer" of 1816. Mary Shelley (Mary Godwin until her marriage in December 1816), her lover and future husband Percy Shelley, and Mary's stepsister Claire Clairmont, spent several months in Switzerland, where they rented a house near the villa where another English traveler, the poet Lord Byron, was staying. One of the most influential literary figures of the early nineteenth century, Byron, accompanied by his physician John Polidori, often entertained the Shelley party at the Villa Diodati near the shores of Lake Geneva. When rainy weather kept the party indoors, they passed the time by reading aloud a collection of German ghost stories. "A playful desire of imitation," recalled Percy Shelley, led Byron to suggest that each person in the group compose a ghost story. Polidori, at odds with his noble employer, devised a story about an aristocratic vampire, which he published as *The Vampyre* in 1819. For her part, Mary Shelley struggled to conceive something original. Then on the evening of June 16, 1816 she experienced a waking dream about "a pale student of unhallowed arts kneeling beside the thing he had put together." She later recalled that she envisioned

> the hideous phantasm of a man stretched out, and then, on the working of some powerful engine, show signs of life, and stir with an uneasy, half vital motion. Frightful must it be; for supremely frightful would be the effect of any human endeavor to mock the stupendous mechanism of the Creator of the world.[1]

With encouragement from Percy Shelley, she spent over a year writing and revising the story that would become *Frankenstein* before submitting it to publishers in England in 1818.

William Godwin (1756–1836)
Caleb Williams
London, 1794
Courtesy Rare Book Room and Special Collections, University Library, University of Illinois at Urbana-Champaign

William Godwin wrote *Caleb Williams,* his best-known novel, while finishing his influential *Enquiry Concerning Political Justice.* Godwin's fiction exemplified his belief in the perfectibility of men through the power of truth and the importance of seeing "things as they are."

William Godwin, 1802
James Northcote (1746–1831)
Photographic reproduction of an oil painting
Courtesy The Granger Collection, New York

William Godwin enjoyed immense fame in the 1790s as a political theorist.

A Writer's Life

As Mary Shelley herself acknowledged, it came as little surprise that she would pursue a literary career. She was the only daughter of two of the most influential and controversial English authors writing in the last decade of the eighteenth century, William Godwin and Mary Wollstonecraft. In the 1790s, Godwin gained fame as the leading English theorist of the French Revolution. During the heady days of the French, American, and Industrial Revolutions, he offered in his treatise *Enquiry Concerning Political Justice* (1793) and in his novel *Caleb Williams* (1794) an ambitious vision of a new political society without governments, crime, or disease.[2]

Mary Wollstonecraft was a writer and political theorist whose *A Vindication of the Rights of Woman* (1792) established her as a major, if iconoclastic, figure. Born in 1759, Wollstonecraft earned her living as a governess before moving to London in 1787 to become a writer. With the support of publisher Joseph Johnson, whose circle of friends included chemist Joseph Priestley, artist Henry Fuseli, political writer Thomas Paine, physician Erasmus Darwin, and other intellectuals, she

Mary Wollstonecraft Godwin, 1797
John Opie (1761–1807)
Photographic reproduction of an engraving
after the painting
Courtesy The Granger Collection, New York

Amid the tumultuous days of the French
Revolution, writer Mary Wollstonecraft
gained notoriety as the author of several
influential and controversial political treatis-
es. She married William Godwin early in
1797, and died eleven days after giving
birth to their daughter Mary.

Mary Wollstonecraft (1759–1797)
A Vindication of the Rights of Woman:
with Strictures on Political and Moral
*Subject*s.
Boston, 1792
Courtesy Library of Congress

This work, for which critics labeled Mary
Wollstonecraft both a "philosophical wan-
ton" and a monster, became an important
text for nineteenth-century feminists.
American reformer and pioneer feminist
Susan B. Anthony presented this copy "of
this earliest work for women's right to equality" to the Library of Congress in 1904.

pursued a successful writing career.3 Within five years, she published *Original
Stories*, compiled *The Female Reader*, and wrote *A Vindication of the Rights of Woman*,
in which she argued in support of women's rights to self-determination and
equality in the intellectual, public, and domestic spheres.4

Mary Wollstonecraft and William Godwin met in 1791 but did not become
lovers until 1797. In his *Enquiry Concerning Political Justice*, Godwin harshly criti-
cized the institution of marriage as a ridiculous convention, noting that the obli-
gation of individuals to live together for an extended period of time must result
in considerable "thwarting, bickering, and great unhappiness."5 Mary
Wollstonecraft, for her part, accepted the necessity of marriage for women. When
she became pregnant in 1797, she and Godwin were married, formalizing their
union on March 29 of that year. Both Wollstonecraft and Godwin wished to provide some legal protection for their unborn child: Wollstonecraft had already
experienced social ostracism as the mother of an illegitimate daughter, the out-
come of an earlier relationship with American entrepreneur Gilbert Imlay. On
August 30, 1797 she gave birth to a daughter, Mary Wollstonecraft Godwin.
Complications with the birth, however, soon brought on the fever feared by all

Percy Shelley, 1819
Amelia Curran (d. 1847)
Photographic reproduction of an oil painting
Courtesy The Granger Collection, New York

Poet and political radical, Percy Shelley was anxious that Mary Shelley prove herself "worthy of her parentage" and eager to see her enroll herself "on the page of fame" through her writing. A more experienced author, he helped prepare *Frankenstein* for publication and supplied the preface for the first edition of the novel.

childbearing women at this time. Mary Wollstonecraft died from puerperal infection September 10, 1797 and was buried in London.

Left with two daughters to raise, Godwin tried to provide a stable domestic life for the children. In 1801 he married Mary Jane Clairmont, a widow with a daughter of her own. Godwin supported his growing family by establishing a publishing house for children's books. He encouraged his young daughter Mary to write; the Godwin Company Juvenile Library published one of her early efforts, a poem "Mounseer Nongtongpaw," when she was only eleven. Despite Godwin's ongoing financial difficulties, his house remained a center of intellectual life in London. He introduced his daughter Mary to such eminent intellectuals as chemist Humphry Davy and American Aaron Burr, as well as the man who would change her life, young poet Percy Shelley.[6]

An ardent admirer of Godwin's political writings, Percy Shelley first visited the Godwin household in 1812. Only recently expelled from Oxford University for publishing a pamphlet *The Necessity of Atheism*, Shelley met fifteen-year-old Mary Godwin when he and his wife Harriet dined with the Godwins in November 1812. Although Mary did not see the poet again for over a year, the two developed an intense romantic attachment when they next met in May 1814. Percy Shelley found her beauty, poetic sensibility, and distinguished parentage extraordinarily attractive. For her part, Mary was attracted to a man, who, like her father, was a passionate revolutionary and philosopher. When William Godwin discovered their relationship in July 1814, he forbade Mary to continue seeing the married Shelley. Ten days later the two lovers fled to France, accompanied by Mary's stepsister, Claire Clairmont. Despite his objections to marriage, Godwin was furious about his daughter's involvement with his young disciple, and refused to have anything to do with the couple. Only after the publication of *Frankenstein* (dedicated to Godwin), the subsequent marriage of Mary and Percy in December 1816, and financial help for the straitened Godwin from Shelley, were good relations restored between father and daughter.

By the summer of 1816, when she began writing *Frankenstein*, nineteen-year-old Mary Shelley had borne Percy two children. Her first child, a daughter born prematurely, died in March 1815. Her second child, William, was born in 1816.

Diodati, The Residence of Lord Byron, 1933
W. Purser
Photographic reproduction of a steel engraving
Courtesy The Granger Collection, New York

During the summer of 1816, Lord Byron rented a villa on the shores of Lake Geneva in Switzerland. Here he proposed the famous ghost-story competition that prompted Mary Shelley to conceive *Frankenstein.*

Lord Byron
William West
Photographic reproduction of an oil painting
Courtesy The Granger Collection, New York

An English romantic poet and political liberal, Byron entertained the Shelley party in Switzerland, where he and Percy engaged in lengthy conversations over the "principle of life," inspiring Mary Shelley's creation of a man who dedicated himself to banishing death.

In December 1816 the death by drowning of Harriet Shelley enabled Mary and Percy Shelley to marry. Before *Frankenstein* was completed, she was pregnant for the third time. The child, Clara, was born in 1817. Of her four children, only one, a son named Percy Florence, survived infancy to reach adulthood. Clara died of fever in 1818, and the three-year-old William died from malaria in 1819, the year Percy Florence was born.[7]

Mary Shelley's tragic losses were not unique in the eighteenth and nineteenth centuries, a time of high rates of maternal, infant, and child mortality. Such losses, however, were unusual among important women writers of these centuries, when most female authors in England and America remained unmarried and childless. Did Mary Shelley's maternal experiences significantly influence her conception of *Frankenstein,* a novel in which a man creates life without the participation of women? Some literary theorists insist that Mary Shelley's pregnancies and losses, as well as the death of her mother following her own birth, materially shaped her writing of the book. "No outside influence need be sought," literary theorist Ellen Moers has argued, "to explain Mary Shelley's fantasy of the newborn as at once monstrous agent of destruction and piteous victim of parental abandonment. 'I, the miserable and the abandoned,' cries the monster at the end of *Frankenstein*, 'I am an abortion to be spurned at, kicked, and trampled on. . .'"[8]

FRANKENSTEIN'S RECEPTION

Mary Shelley published her novel anonymously in March 1818. *Frankenstein; or, The Modern Prometheus*, printed in three volumes, received mostly positive reviews from critics, and the first run of five hundred copies, for which the author received a total of twenty-eight pounds, sold well.[9] Novelist Sir Walter Scott praised the clarity and vigor of the author's originality and language, although he challenged some of the improbabilities of the monster's self-education, including his reading Goethe, Plutarch, and John Milton's *Paradise Lost*.[10] A few reviewers were far more critical of the "tissue of horrible and disgusting absurdity" presented in the work, and its failure to provide a useful, moral lesson.[11]

The identity of the anonymous author prompted some speculation among critics. Most people assumed that it was a man, given the subject matter and the quality of the writing. Walter Scott was among those who believed, given the anonymous author's dedication of the book to William Godwin, that Percy Shelley had written the novel. (Percy Shelley had, in fact, reviewed the novel before publication and contributed the preface to the first edition.) Annoyed by this misapprehension, Mary Shelley wrote to Scott in June 1818, absolving her husband of any responsibility for her own "juvenile attempt."[12] Long after her authorship was known, literary critics continued to give Percy rather than Mary Shelley credit for her achievement. "Nothing but an absolute magnetizing of her brain by Shelley's," the 1897 edition of the *Dictionary of National Biography* dismissively observed, "can account for her having risen so far above her usual self

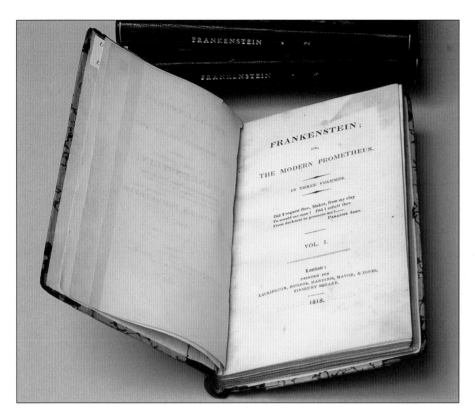

Mary Shelley (1797–1851)
Frankenstein; or, The Modern Prometheus, Vols. 1–3
London, 1818
Courtesy Singer-Mendenhall Collection, Annenberg Rare Book and Manuscript Library, University of Pennsylvania

The London printer Lackington issued the novel, which appeared without Mary Shelley's name, in three volumes. Most novel sales at the time were made to private lending libraries, which circulated their books among fee-paying customers. Thus, a novel published in three parts could be loaned to three different patrons.

as in 'Frankenstein.'"[13] Although *Frankenstein* has remained in print since the early nineteenth century, only in the last two decades has Mary Shelley received serious consideration as an author rather than merely the wife of Percy Shelley.

In the four years following the publication of *Frankenstein*, Mary Shelley weathered several crises. Her fifth pregnancy, which ended in miscarriage in

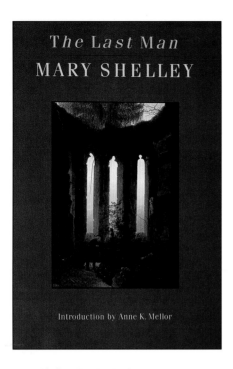

Mary Shelley (1797–1851)
The Last Man
University of Nebraska Press, Lincoln,
Nebraska, 1993
Courtesy Stephen J. Greenberg

Like her mother, whose own father wasted away the family fortune, Mary Shelley was compelled, after Percy's death, to write to support herself and her young son. In addition to novels, she wrote travel books, short fiction, and entries for encyclopedias. Her novel *The Last Man* in which Englishman Lionel Verney is the sole survivor of a twenty-first century plague, was condemned in Mary Shelley's time as "the product of a diseased imagination and a polluted taste." This novel, as well as many of her other works, are still available today.

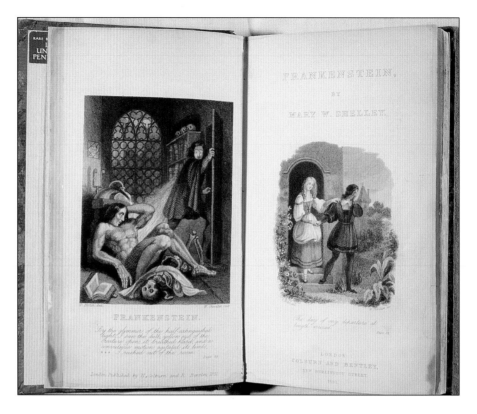

Mary Shelley (1797–1851)
Frankenstein; or, The Modern Prometheus
London, 1831
Courtesy Singer-Mendenhall Collection, Annenberg Rare Book and Manuscript Library, University of Pennsylvania

For the 1831 edition, Mary Shelley wrote a new preface and made several changes in the text. She continued to have great affection for her "hideous progeny," the "offspring of happy days" before the deaths of her children, William and Clara, and of her husband.

1822, nearly cost her her life when she experienced massive bleeding. Her husband saved her by placing her in an ice bath in order to stop the hemorrhaging.[14] The same year, Percy Shelley died in an accident at sea. His death at age thirty compelled Mary Shelley to support herself and her one surviving child with her writing. In addition to travel essays and encyclopedia entries, she edited Percy Shelley's poetry and wrote a number of novels, including a historical romance,

Valperga (1823), an apocalyptic novel set in the plague-desolated twenty-first century, *The Last Man* (1826), another historical romance, *The Fortunes of Perkin Warbeck* (1830), and two domestic romances, *Lodore* (1835) and *Falkner* (1837).[15] In 1831 Mary Shelley published a revised edition of *Frankenstein* with a new introduction. Although she received several proposals, she never remarried after Percy's death. Mary Shelley died in 1851.

BOUNDARY CROSSINGS IN 1818

In the introduction to the 1831 edition of *Frankenstein*, Mary Shelley reminisced that she was often asked how so young a girl "came to think of, and to dilate upon, so very hideous an idea?" She provided her own account of the origins of the idea of "bestowing animation on lifeless matter." Recalling a conversation between Lord Byron and Percy Shelley on the nature of the "principle of life," including an experiment by Erasmus Darwin in which a piece of vermicelli (a type of worm) preserved in a glass jar began to move with a voluntary motion, she explained: "I speak not of what the Doctor really did, or said that he did, but as more to my purpose, of what was then spoken of as having been done by him." She went on to speculate that "perhaps a corpse would be re-animated; galvanism had given token of such things; perhaps the component parts of a creature might be manufactured, brought together, and endued with vital warmth."[16]

In the early nineteenth century the boundary between life and death, between the organic and inorganic world, intrigued many students of nature. Physicians and natural philosophers like Erasmus Darwin supported the idea that living organisms could develop from non-living matter, a process known as spontaneous generation. In *The Temple of Nature*, Erasmus Darwin discussed experiments in which lower organisms developed spontaneously from vegetable or animal materials, describing how some "gentlemen put some boiling veal broth into a phial previously heated in the fire, and sealing it hermetically or with melted wax, observed it to be replete with animalcules in three or four days." Darwin also noted how "in a paste composed of flour and water . . . the animalcules called eels" were seen in great abundance and possessed a vigorous

Erasmus Darwin (1731–1802)
The Temple of Nature; or, The Origin of Society
Baltimore, 1804

A poet, physician, and botanist, Erasmus Darwin wrote extensively on the natural world. In the philosophical notes which accompanied this lengthy poem, Darwin described some research into spontaneous generation that may have influenced Mary Shelley in composing *Frankenstein*. Artist Henry Fuseli, once romantically linked to Mary Wollstonecraft, contributed the frontispiece for the book.

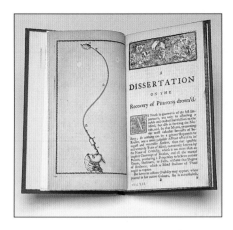

Rowland Jackson (d. ca. 1787)
A Physical Dissertation on Drowning
London, 1747

In the second half of the eighteenth century, humane societies operated receiving stations where members attempted to revive persons found drowned. Using such devices as the resuscitation bellows (illustrated above), the London Society claimed to have revived more than two thousand people by 1796.

motion.[17] It wasn't until the late nineteenth century that chemist Louis Pasteur and others disproved the theory of spontaneous generation.[18]

In addition to the spontaneous generation of lower organisms, physicians in the late eighteenth and early nineteenth century devoted considerable attention to resuscitating the apparently dead. Beginning in the 1760s, "humane societies," organized by physicians and other reformers, began to teach methods to revive the drowned or suffocated. Using smelling salts, vigorous shaking and other manipulations, artificial respiration, and especially electricity, these societies reported dramatic success: the London Society, organized in 1774, boasted of reviving more than two thousand people by 1796.[19] When Harriet Shelley, Percy's first wife, was found drowned in the Serpentine Lake in 1816, rescuers took her body to a receiving station of the London Society, where resuscitation efforts were unsuccessful. Medical writers like American physician David Ramsey sensed the dawn of a new age of medical power: "How many must have been lost to their friends and community," he inquired in 1801, "before mankind were acquainted with the god-like art of restoring suspended animation?"[20] Mary Shelley's own experiences suggest a personal interest in the god-like power of reanimation. In a diary entry for March 1815, she recorded a disturbing dream in which her dead child, a daughter, was revived by being rubbed before a fire.[21]

One of the dramatic new techniques for reviving the nearly dead was blood transfusion. First introduced in the seventeenth century following English physician William Harvey's demonstration of the circulation of the blood, early transfusions involved the transfer of blood from animals (lambs) to humans, a practice largely abandoned by the early eighteenth century. In the early nineteenth century London physician James Blundell introduced human-to-human transfusion as a desperate measure to revive women who experienced massive hemorrhaging following childbirth.[22] Blundell devised a "gravitator" made of brass which he used to funnel blood from a standing donor to a reclining recipient. The medical journal *The Lancet* recorded the dramatic success of this procedure. After a woman received two and one-half ounces of her husband's blood, the journal noted, "Life seemed to be immediately reanimated as by an electric spark."[23]

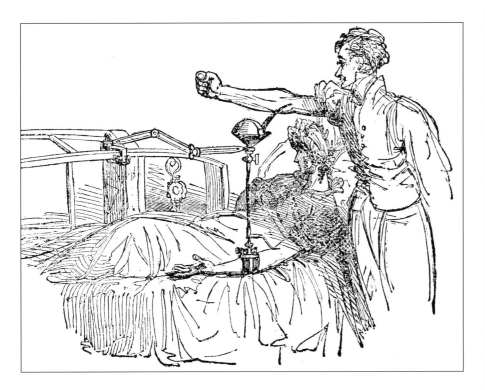

Blundell's Gravitator
Artist unknown
Photographic reproduction of an illustration appearing in *The Lancet,* 1828–1829
Courtesy Pennsylvania State University Libraries

After its invention, James Blundell continued to improve his transfusion device. In 1828 he described the gravitator, which could be used to transmit blood in a "regulated stream" from one individual to another.

Blood transfusion apparatus
Made by James Blundell
London, 1819
Courtesy International Museum of Surgical Science, Chicago, IL

English physician James Blundell introduced human-to-human transfusion in an effort to save the lives of the near-dead. He devised a copper cup with a metal handle to collect blood. After witnessing a woman receiving blood from her husband, one observer noted "Life seemed to be immediately reanimated as by an electric spark."

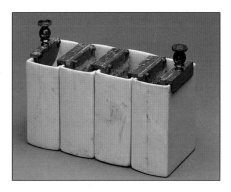

Crown of cups battery
Made by W.H. Halse
England, ca. 1865
Courtesy The Bakken

Alessandro Volta proposed two methods for the generation of electrical current, the crown of cups and the voltaic pile. The crown of cups consists of porcelain cups containing a brine solution in which pairs of metal plates (zinc and silver or copper) are suspended.

The direct application of electricity, or *galvanism*, to revive the dead generated intense interest among physicians and the public. In the 1780s and 1790s Luigi Galvani, professor of anatomy at the University of Bologna, performed an extensive series of studies in which he applied a bimetallic arc between a dissected frog leg muscle and the frog's crural nerve, producing movement. These demonstrations confirmed for Galvani that animals possessed a subtle "nerveo electrical fluid," a form of "animal electricity." Dismissing Galvani's experiments as "unbelievable," his countryman, physicist Alessandro Volta, argued that Galvani's arc, not his frog preparation, was the source of electricity.[24] To increase

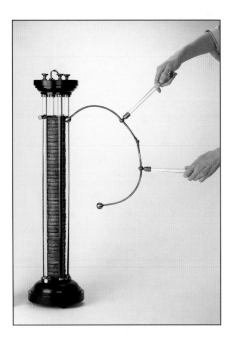

Voltaic pile
French (?), ca. 19th century
Conducting arc
English (?), ca. 1820
Courtesy The Bakken

In 1800 Alessandro Volta described the voltaic pile. Constructed of alternating discs of zinc and copper, with pieces of cardboard soaked in brine between the metals, the pile produced electrical current. The metallic conducting arc was used to carry the electricity over a greater distance.

this "electromotive force," Volta created a battery or pile (the voltaic pile) and the "crown of cups," which he announced in 1800. A medium-sized pile (constructed of forty or fifty pairs of zinc and copper disks separated by pieces of moist cardboard) produced an electrical discharge in a person holding both ends of the pile, a sensation similar to one experienced upon grasping an electrical fish.[25]

Public demonstrations of the effects of electricity on animal and human bodies—living and dead—attracted large audiences across Europe. Galvani's nephew, physician Giovanni Aldini, for example, performed extensive demonstrations for popular audiences. In 1802 and 1803, he conducted a series of demonstrations in London, including one for the Prince of Wales, in which he applied electrical current to the ears and nose of a newly decapitated ox head. To the astonishment of the crowd, the application caused the eyes of the ox to open, the tongue to be agitated, and shaking of the nose and tongue.[26] In 1803, Aldini administered an electrical current to the body of a murderer executed at Newgate Prison. Upon initial administration of the current to the face, "the jaw of the deceased criminal began to quiver, and the adjoining muscles were horribly contorted, and one eye was actually opened."[27] In further experiments with the bodies of the dead, Aldini successfully produced movement in the corpses. These demonstrations, using the decapitated heads of dogs, oxen, and human beings, were widely replicated in England and Europe. Although concern about such demonstrations led the Prussian government in 1804 to issue an edict forbidding the use of decapitated criminals' heads in galvanic experiments, experiments on executed criminals continued in Britain.[28] When Andrew Ure "galvanized" the body of an executed murderer in Glasgow in November 1818, he recorded the dramatic effect:

> Every muscle in his countenance was simultaneously thrown into fearful action; rage, horror, despair, anguish, and ghastly smiles, united their hideous expression in the murderer's face, surpassing far the wildest representations of a Fuseli or a Kean.[29]

During this time of electrical experimentation, *Frankenstein* made its first appearance. Although the contraction of muscles produced in corpses by means

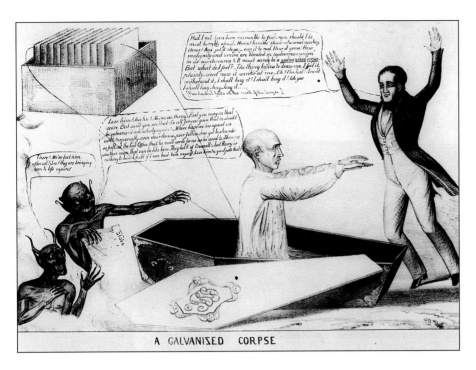

A Galvanized Corpse, 1836
Henry R. Robinson
Photographic reproduction of a lithograph
Courtesy Library of Congress

Galvanism captured popular attention on both sides of the Atlantic. In this 1836 American political cartoon, Jacksonian newspaper editor Francis Preston Blair rises from the grave after receiving a jolt from a galvanic battery.

of electrical energy was not evidence of life in the way we understand it today, such movements signaled the radical potential of this new technology, and the Promethean possibility that life itself could be restored. Mary Shelley herself recalled listening to conversations between Lord Byron and Percy Shelley about the possibility of reanimating dead bodies, in light of the developments in galvanism and animal electricity.

Plate 2
Artist unknown
Photographic reproduction of an illustration from
Giovanni Aldini (1762–1834), *An Account of the Late
Improvements in Galvanism,* 1803

Italian physician Giovanni Aldini used a voltaic pile for
his demonstrations of the effects of electrical current on
the bodies of animals and humans.

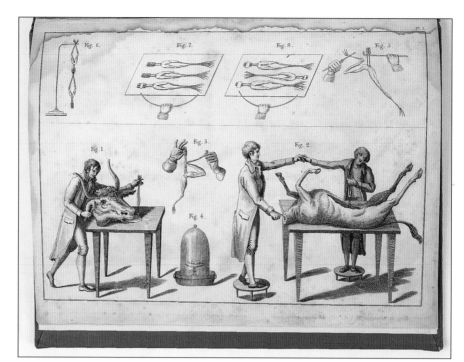

Galvanic Experiments
Artist unknown
Photographic reproduction of an engraving from
Giovanni Aldini (1762–1834), *Essai Théorique et
Expérimentale sur le Galvanisme,* 1804

In his book *Essai Théorique et Expérimentale sur le
Galvanisme,* Giovanni Aldini described some of the public demonstrations in which he applied electricity to the
bodies of newly executed criminals. The application of
electrical current produced twitching of the eye and
other movements.

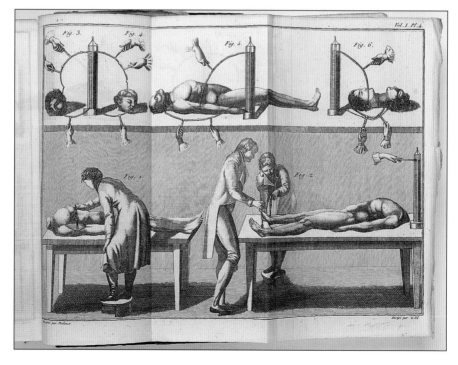

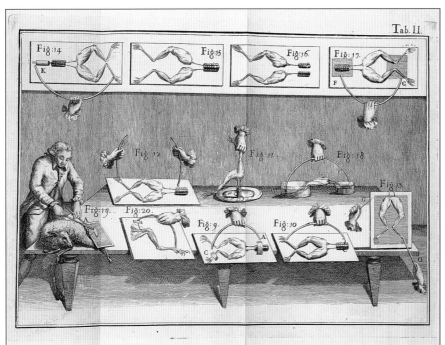

Table II
Artist unknown
Photographic reproduction of an engraving from Luigi Galvani (1737–1798), *De Viribus Electricitatis in Motu Musculari*, 1792

Electricity excited much wonder in the eighteenth century. Physician Luigi Galvani described the "constant and wonderful phenomenon" of the frog's remote contraction in his studies of animal electricity.

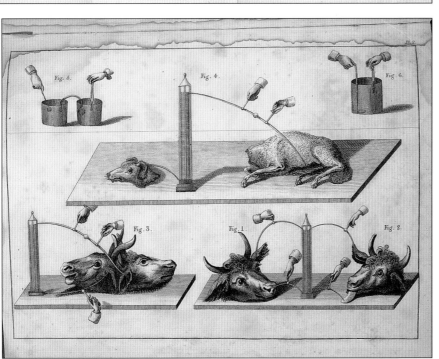

Plate 1
Artist unknown
Photographic reproduction of an illustration from Giovanni Aldini (1762–1834), *An Account of the Late Improvements in Galvanism*, 1803

Victor's Midnight Labors, 1984
Barry Moser (b. 1940)
Photographic reproduction of a wood engraving from *Frankenstein; or, The Modern Prometheus,* Pennyroyal Press, 1984
Courtesy Barry Moser

One of the unsettling elements of the Frankenstein story and the one element that endures in each retelling of the tale is the "raw" material that the young Victor used to create the monster. In the novel, Mary Shelley described how Frankenstein "dabbled among the unhallowed damps of the grave, or tortured the living animal to animate the lifeless clay."[30] In addition to harvesting his raw materials from the cemetery, Frankenstein collected bones from charnel houses (where bones were collected and stored), and frequented slaughterhouses and the dissecting rooms of hospitals to acquire the body parts he needed to assemble his creature.

Mary Shelley's terrifying vision of a pale student assembling a man out of body parts collected from the graveyard and dissecting rooms vividly parallels the public demonstrations by physicians in which decapitated human bodies, frog legs, and ox heads moved in response to electrical stimuli. Although her character Victor Frankenstein explains that he experiences no supernatural horror with his investigations into the corruption of the human body after it becomes "food for the worm," Mary Shelley knew that some of her readers would recoil at such passages.[31] In the early nineteenth century, anatomical studies like those conducted by Victor Frankenstein generated public hostility in light of the methods physicians and surgeons used to acquire the necessary "material" for study. Before the revised edition of *Frankenstein* was published in 1831, the only bodies legally available to physicians and surgeons for anatomical dissection were those of executed criminals; indeed, public dissection was a culminating feature of their punishment. This irregular and inadequate supply of corpses prompted some physicians to engage in body-snatching or to hire "resurrectionists" to obtain the dead bodies they needed for research. Between the first edition of *Frankenstein* in 1818 and the revised 1831 edition, a number of eminent London physicians actively campaigned for a law to make the bodies of unclaimed hospital and workhouse inmates legally available for anatomical dissection; they were pleased by the passage of the Anatomy Act enacted by the British Parliament in 1832.[32]

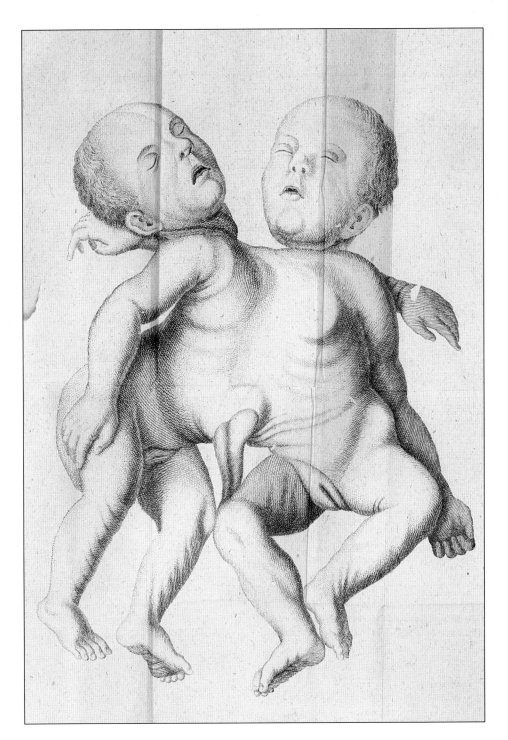

Albrecht von Haller (1708–1777)
Opuscula sua Anatomica de Respiratione, de Monstris Alique Minora
Göttingen, 1751

In the 1750s Swiss anatomist Albrecht von Haller argued in support of preformation, a theory of generation in which the organism exists preformed in the germ. For Haller, monstrous structures like these conjoined infants did not develop but were preformed.

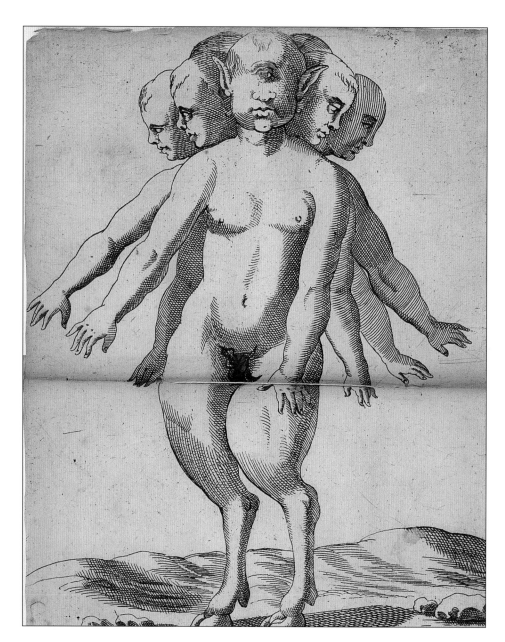

Jean Riolan (1580–1657)
De Monstro Nato Lutetiae Anno Domini. 1605.
Paris, 1605

Victor Frankenstein created a "miserable monster" even though he took pains to select beautiful features. In the seventeenth and eighteenth centuries, physicians sought to classify
and explain the origins of monsters and monstrous births.

In her novel, Mary Shelley described how the young Victor Frankenstein exercised "infinite pains and care" in selecting beautiful features for the lifeless thing he had endeavored to form. Despite this care, he produced a hideous, living "abortion," a monster, rather than a well-formed human creature. The question of how monsters, deviations from normal human development, originated interested many physicians in the eighteenth and nineteenth centuries. In his entry on monsters in an 1819 English encyclopedia, London physician William Lawrence, who treated both Percy and Mary Shelley, observed that "Particular bodily formations, particular mental characters, and dispositions to certain diseases, are transmitted to offspring. . . . We ascribe then the aberrations from the usual form and structure of the body, which produce monsters, to an irregular operation of the powers concerned in generation." His own personal interest in human deviations prompted Lawrence to foster an "abnormal child" or "monster" in order to study its development.[33] Books on anatomy and generation featured images of these deviations from normal development, as physicians sought explanations for such occurrences.[34] In *Frankenstein* the monster's ugliness and his enormous stature (the creature is eight feet tall) violently repel all who encounter him, including, most disastrously, his own creator. Victor Frankenstein abandons his "miserable monster" upon seeing his "hideous yellow skin, watery eyes, shrivelled complexion, and straight, black lips."[35]

Mary Shelley's own interest in monstrosity and "gruesome" anatomical detail is suggested by her visits to museums of natural history, which displayed wax models of the human body. In 1820, for example, she recorded in her journal a visit to the Gabinetto Fisico, a well-known Italian museum, whose collections included "gruesome" wax models of the pregnant human uterus. "This awful region, which should be sacred to men of science, is open to all," complained Joseph Forsyth, author of the guidebook Mary Shelley read in preparation for her visit to the museum. "Nay, the very apartment where the gravid uterus and its processes lie unveiled, is a favorite lounge of the ladies, who criticise aloud all the mysteries of sex."[36]

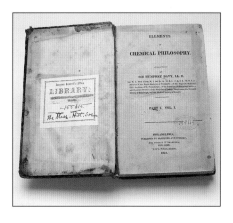

Sir Humphry Davy (1778–1829)
Elements of Chemical Philosophy, Part 1, Vol. 1
Philadelphia, 1812

Both Mary and Percy Shelley were interested in the works of Humphry Davy, who was a friend of Mary's father, William Godwin. Davy's demonstrations on chemical phenomena attracted large popular audiences. In the introduction to this work, Davy mentioned two alchemical philosophers (Paracelsus and Cornelius Agrippa), whose works inspired the young Victor Frankenstein.

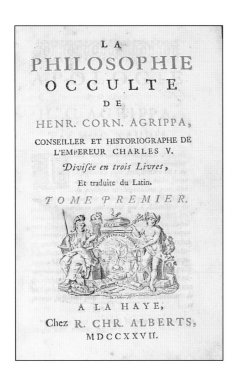

Heinrich Cornelius Agrippa von Nettesheim
(1486–1535)
La Philosophie Occulte, Vols. 1 & 2
La Haye, 1727

In this text, the most widely used and respected of all books on the magical arts, Cornelius Agrippa combined Christian theology with the cabala, an occult religious strain of Judaism. In *Frankenstein,* young Victor Frankenstein reads the whole works of Cornelius Agrippa hoping to master a "secret store of knowledge" about the natural world.

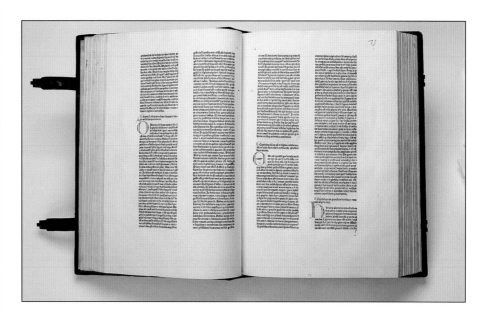

Saint Albertus Magnus (1193?–1280)
De Animalibus
Mantua, 1479

In his youth, Victor Frankenstein called himself a disciple of Albertus Magnus. Saint Albertus Magnus introduced Greek and Arab science into the universities of the Middle Ages. Although he repudiated magic and astrology in his own works, he came to be regarded as a powerful magician.

ALCHEMY AND MODERN SCIENCE

After meeting Percy Shelley, Mary Shelley embarked on an ambitious reading program, which included works of philosophy, natural science, and history. On her reading list in the fall of 1816, for example, was Humphry Davy's *Elements of Chemical Philosophy* (1812).[37] A professor of chemistry at the Royal Institution in London, Davy attracted large audiences to his scientific lectures; in 1810 more than ten thousand people flocked to see his demonstrations on electrochemistry and other topics.[38] In the *Elements of Chemical Philosophy,* Davy chronicled the progress of chemistry from the alchemy of the Renaissance through developments occurring in the early nineteenth century.[39] In *Frankenstein,* Mary Shelley invoked the alchemical tradition exemplified in the works of Renaissance

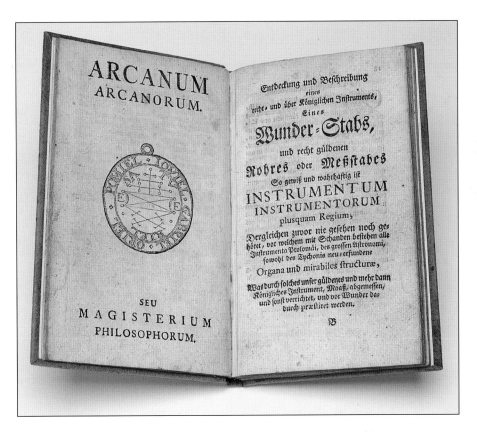

Paracelsus (1493–1541)
Philippi Theophrasti Bombast von Hohenheim Paracelsi Genannt, Geheimniss aller seiner Geheimnisse, welches noch niemahls Wegen seiner unverglaichlichen Furtreflichkeit ist Gemein gemacht
Frankfurt, 1770

During his study at the University of Ingolstadt, Victor Frankenstein apprenticed himself to Professor Waldman who praised Agrippa and Paracelsus as "men whose indefatigable zeal provided the foundations of modern knowledge." A physician and mystic, Paracelsus helped bridge Renaissance alchemy and modern chemistry. His views encompassed both astrological medicine and a new theory of disease causation.

philosophers Albertus Magnus, Cornelius Agrippa, and Paracelsus by having Victor Frankenstein read their texts in his youth. In her novel both the alchemical pursuit of the elixir of life and the developments of modern science merge in Frankenstein's search for the perfectibility of the human body and the victory over corruption and death.[40]

Frankenstein: The Modern Prometheus

Prometheus Bound, 1611–1612
Peter Paul Rubens (1577–1640)
Photographic reproduction of an oil painting
Courtesy The Granger Collection, New York

Mary Shelley drew on a large number of sources—scientific, literary, experiential—in conceiving her pale student and his monstrous creation. Although some readers both in her own time and today have read the book as a simple primer about the dangers of unvaunted scientific ambition, the subtitle of her novel "The Modern Prometheus" suggests a more ambiguous rendering of the potential dangers and benefits of penetrating the secrets of nature. Frankenstein could be considered a benefactor of humankind; his desire to "renew life where death had apparently devoted the body to corruption" was a vision he shared with other medical Prometheans of the early nineteenth century. According to Greek mythology, Prometheus created humankind out of mud and water. He angered the gods by stealing fire from the heavens to give to humans. As a punishment for his daring, Zeus sentenced Prometheus to be chained to a rock where an eagle or vulture would daily devour his liver. In the eighteenth century, the physical dangers of researching electricity were quickly linked to the Prometheus myth. In 1753, when G.W. Richmann died during a thunderstorm while conducting experiments into electricity, the *Gentlemen's Magazine* noted "we are come at last to touch the celestial fire, which if . . . we make too free with, as it is fabled Prometheus did of old, like him we may be brought too late to repent of our temerity."[41]

Paradise Lost

The Expulsion from Eden, 17th century
Artist unknown
Photographic reproduction of a line engraving
Courtesy The Granger Collection, New York

Did I request thee, Maker, from my clay
To mould me man? Did I solicit thee
From darkness to promote me?—

> Lines from John Milton's *Paradise Lost*
> From the title page of *Frankenstein; or,*
> *The Modern Prometheus,* 1818

In *Frankenstein*, the intelligent and sensitive monster created by Victor Frankenstein reads a copy of Milton's *Paradise Lost*, which profoundly stirs his emotions. The monster compares his situation to that of Adam. Unlike the first man who had "come forth from the hands of God a perfect creature," Frankenstein's creature is hideously formed. Abandoned by Victor Frankenstein, the monster finds himself "wretched, helpless, and alone."

Surrounded by Ice

Untitled, 1827
Artist unknown
Photographic reproduction of an engraving
from *Northern Exposure,* 1827
Courtesy Picture Collection, The Branch Libraries,
The New York Public Library

A sledge . . . had drifted towards us in the night, on a large fragment of ice. Only one dog remained alive; but there was a human being within it. . . . His limbs were nearly frozen, and his body dreadfully emaciated by fatigue and suffering. I never saw a man in so wretched a condition.

> Robert Walton to his sister Mrs. Saville
> *Frankenstein; or, The Modern Promethues,*
> 1818

Frankenstein opens with a series of letters written by Arctic explorer Robert Walton, engaged in a personal quest to expand the boundaries of the known world. It is Walton who first encounters Victor Frankenstein in the Arctic desperately searching for the monster he has created. The explorer becomes the only person to hear Victor Frankenstein's strange and tragic tale.

The Spark of Life

The Blasted Stump, 1984
Barry Moser (b. 1940)
Photographic reproduction of a wood engraving from *Frankenstein; or, The Modern Prometheus,* Pennyroyal Press, 1984
Courtesy Barry Moser

I beheld a stream of fire issue from an old and beautiful oak . . . and so soon as the dazzling light vanished, the oak had disappeared, and nothing remained but a blasted stump. . . . I eagerly inquired of my father the nature and origin of thunder and lightning. He replied, "Electricity."

> Victor Frankenstein to Robert Walton
> *Frankenstein; or, The Modern Prometheus,*
> 1818

In Mary Shelley's day, many people regarded the new science of electricity with both wonder and astonishment. In *Frankenstein*, Shelley used both the new sciences of chemistry and electricity and the older Renaissance tradition of the alchemist's search for the elixir of life to conjure up the Promethean possibility of reanimating the bodies of the dead.

Unveiling the Recesses of Nature

Midnight Labors

Experiment with an Air-Pump, ca. 1768
Joseph Wright (1734–1797)
Photographic reproduction of an oil painting
Courtesy The Granger Collection, New York

The modern masters promise very little. . . . But these philosophers . . . have indeed performed miracles. They have discovered how the blood circulates, and the nature of the air we breathe. They have acquired new and almost unlimited powers; they can command the thunders of heaven, mimic the earthquake, and even mock the invisible world with its own shadows.

Professor Waldman to his class at the University of Ingolstadt
Frankenstein; or, The Modern Prometheus, 1818

By the early nineteenth century, philosophers like physician Erasmus Darwin and chemist Humphry Davy, both well known to Mary Shelley, pointed the way to mastery of the physical universe. Discoveries about the human body and the natural world promised the dawn of a new age of medical power, when such things as reanimation of dead tissue and the end of death and disease seemed within reach.

And the Red Death Held Illimitable Dominion Over All, 1969
Federico Castellon
Photographic reproduction of a lithograph

Who shall conceive the horrors of my secret toil, as I dabbled among the unhallowed damps of the grave, or tortured the living animal to animate the lifeless clay?

Victor Frankenstein
Frankenstein; or, The Modern Prometheus, 1818

With feverish excitement, Victor Frankenstein pursues nature to her hiding places. By moonlight, he gathers the body parts he needs by visits to the graveyard, to the charnel house, to the hospital dissecting room, and the slaughterhouse. Although he finds his solitary preoccupation repulsive, he is not deterred from his quest to restore life.

Hideous Progeny

Untitled, 1779
J.F. Declassan
Photographic reproduction of an illustration from Jacques Gamelin (1739–1803), *Nouveau Recueil d'Osteologie et de Myologie*, 1779

I collected the instruments of life around me, that I might infuse a spark of being into the lifeless thing that lay at my feet. . . . His yellow skin scarcely covered the work of muscles and arteries beneath; his hair was of a lustrous black, and flowing . . . [it] formed a more horrid contrast with his watery eyes, that seemed almost of the same colour as the dun white sockets in which they were set, his shrivelled complexion, and straight black lips.

> Victor Frankenstein
> *Frankenstein; or, The Modern Prometheus,*
> 1818

Overcome by the horror of what he has done, Victor Frankenstein abandons the "miserable monster" he fathered in his laboratory. That evening a nightmare disturbs his sleep; Elizabeth, his fiancée, becomes in his arms the decaying corpse of his own dead mother. The next morning when he returns to his "workshop of filthy creation," the monster has escaped.

Poor, Helpless, Miserable Wretch

Madness, or A Man Bound with Chains
Artist unknown
Photographic reproduction from an illustration from Sir Charles Bell (1774–1842), *Essays on the Anatomy of Expression in Painting*, 1806

But where were my friends and relations? No father had watched my infant days, no mother had blessed me with smiles and caresses; or if they had, all my past life was now a blot, a blind vacancy in which I distinguished nothing. From my earliest remembrance I had been as I then was in height and proportion. I had never yet seen a being resembling me. . . . What was I?

> The Monster
> *Frankenstein; or, The Modern Prometheus,*
> 1818

Mary Shelley gave her monster feelings and intelligence. Fatherless and motherless, the monster struggles to find his place in human society, struggles with the most fundamental questions of identity and personal history. Alone, he learns to speak, to read, and to ponder "his accursed origins." All the while, he suffers from the loneliness of never seeing anyone resembling himself.

Remaining Silent

Finis, 1733
Artist unknown
Photographic reproduction of an engraving from William Cheselden (1688–1752), *Osteographia, or, The Anatomy of the Bones*, 1733

I paused when I reflected on the story that I had to tell. A being whom I myself had formed, and endued with life, had met me at midnight among the precipices. . . . I well knew that if any other had communicated such a relation to me, I should have looked upon it as the ravings of insanity. Besides, the strange nature of the animal would elude all pursuit, even if I were so far credited as to persuade my relatives to commence it. . . . I resolved to remain silent.

> Victor Frankenstein
> *Frankenstein; or, The Modern Prometheus,*
> 1818

Abandoned by his creator, the monster takes his revenge by killing Victor Frankenstein's younger brother, William. Frankenstein's silence, in the face of the monster's murderous actions, exacts a terrible price. His self-imposed isolation from society mirrors the social isolation the monster experiences from all who see him. Frankenstein's decision to remain silent about the monster leads to further tragedy.

A Monstrous Mate

The Nightmare, 1781
Henry Fuseli (1741–1825)
Photographic reproduction of an oil painting on canvas
Courtesy Founders Society Purchase with funds from Mr. and Mrs. Bert L. Smokler and Mr. and Mrs. Lawrence A. Fleischman. Photograph ©1997 The Detroit Institute of Arts

> I demand a creature of another sex, but as hideous as myself. . . . It is true, we shall be monsters, cut off from all the world; but on that account we shall be more attached to one another. Our lives will not be happy, but they will be harmless, and free from the misery I now feel. Oh! my creator, make me happy; let me feel gratitude toward you for one benefit! Let me see that I excite the sympathy of some existing thing; do not deny me my request!
>
> The monster to Victor Frankenstein
> *Frankenstein; or, The Modern Prometheus,* 1818

Victor Frankenstein initially agrees to create a mate for his monster. But as Frankenstein begins to assemble an Eve for his Adam, he grows terrified by the prospect that this female creature will be "ten thousand times more malignant" than her companion, and that the two might themselves produce "a race of devils." Breaking his promise to the monster, Frankenstein disposes of the body parts he gathered to produce the female creature. Inflamed with hatred, the monster sets out to destroy in Frankenstein's life all that he coveted for his own. After killing Clerval, Frankenstein's best friend, the monster murders Elizabeth, Frankenstein's bride, on their wedding night.

The Greatness of His Fall

Broussais
Charles Blanc
Photographic reproduction of an etching

> The forms of the beloved death flit before me, and I hasten to their arms. Farewell, Walton! Seek happiness in tranquility, and avoid ambition, even if it be only the apparently innocent one of distinguishing yourself in science and discoveries. Yet why do I say this? I have myself been blasted in these hopes, yet another may succeed.
>
> Victor Frankenstein to explorer
> Robert Walton
> *Frankenstein; or, The Modern Prometheus,*
> 1818

As he lies dying aboard Walton's ship, Victor Frankenstein offers an ambivalent assessment of his own conduct. In both the subtitle (*The Modern Prometheus*) of her novel and through Frankenstein's dying words, Mary Shelley suggests that Frankenstein's misfortune did not arise from his Promethean ambition of creating life, but from the mistreatment of his creature. Frankenstein's failure to assume responsibility for the miserable wretch he fathered in his workshop is his real tragedy.

Monstrous Remorse

Hiob (Job)
Artist unknown
Photographic reproduction of a halftone
reproduction of a woodcut

Once I falsely hoped to meet with beings, who, pardoning my outward form, would love me for the excellent qualities which I was capable of bringing forth. I was nourished with high thoughts of honour and devotion. But now vice has degraded me beneath the meanest animal. . . . The fallen angel becomes a malignant devil. . . . I am quite alone.

The monster to explorer Robert Walton
Frankenstein; or, The Modern Prometheus, 1818

Encountering Robert Walton aboard his ship, the monster expresses overwhelming remorse for his frightful catalogue of misdeeds, the deaths of William, Clerval, Elizabeth, and his creator. The creature informs the explorer that he will destroy himself in the frozen north, and disappears in the icy waves. The tragedy of Victor Frankenstein and his monster is complete.

Frankenstein, 1931

Courtesy Museum of Modern Art/Film Stills Archive Reproduced courtesy Universal Studios Licensing, Inc.

THE CELLULOID MONSTER

In the twentieth century, popular culture on both sides of the Atlantic embraced the Frankenstein story and maintained it in such a way that references to "Frankenstein" are immediately recognizable to a broad range of people. As early as 1823, Mary Shelley's novel began a transformation that would reach its culmination in 1931 on the silver screen, when the image of Boris Karloff came to define popular images of the Frankenstein monster. In this transformation, the creature would lose much of the complexity which Mary Shelley gave him. From a sensitive, reasoning, and articulate being whose crimes result from his treatment at the hands of humanity, the creature was transformed into a grunting brute whose cruelty can only be understood as the product of his maker's daring to usurp the god-like power of creation. Creative and commercial artists have used this simplified and distorted formula to represent the Frankenstein monster in hundreds of films, television programs, and consumer products. Why and how do the Frankenstein monster and myth continue to exert a powerful hold on our collective imaginations? Part of the answer lies in the assurance that the myth gives of punishing those who transgress natural and divine laws. Amid the tumultuous changes in politics and science, such unambiguous assurances offer both comfort and stability.

ESCAPING SHELLEY'S FRAME

In her 1831 introduction to *Frankenstein*, Mary Shelley bid her "hideous progeny" to go forth into the world. By that time, she was well aware that her novel had already escaped her control. In 1823 she learned from her father of an upcoming English Opera House performance of *Presumption; or, The Fate of Frankenstein* by London playwright Richard Brinsley Peake. The production, according to the playbill, emphasized the "striking moral of the story," namely "the fatal consequences of that presumption, which attempts to penetrate, beyond prescribed depths, into the mysteries of nature."[42]

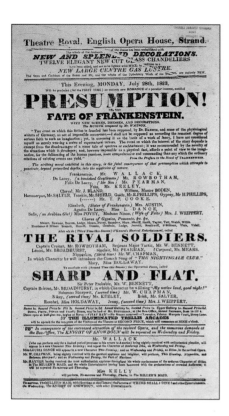

**Playbill from opening night of *Presumption;
or, The Fate of Frankenstein*,** July 28, 1823,
London
*Bequest of Evert Jansen Wendell, The Harvard
Theatre Collection, The Houghton Library*

Mary Shelley attended a performance of
Presumption at the Royal English Opera House
on August 29, 1823. "The play bill amused me
extremely," she wrote a friend, "for in the list of
dramatis personae came,— by Mr. T. Cooke;
this nameless mode of naming the unameable
[sic] is rather good."

In adapting the novel for the stage, Peake made a series of changes that others would follow in streamlining Shelley's complex and ambiguous story for popular consumption. Most importantly, the playwright transformed the monster from Mary Shelley's eloquent and well-read storyteller into a speechless creature who kills without reason or remorse. Peake also eliminated a number of characters from the novel, most prominently Arctic polar explorer Robert Walton who finds Victor Frankenstein on the ice and listens to his tale. At the same time, Peake introduced the character of the scientist's laboratory assistant, who functioned as both a comic foil and narrator of the play's action.

Presumption excited both popularity and controversy. A series of protests by the London Society for the Prevention of Vice condemned the play for its "attack on the Christian faith" and the attempts to "burlesque the resurrection of the dead."[43] Nearly all condemnations of the play alluded to the play's connections with Percy Shelley and his circle. The efforts to suppress the performances, however, did little to hurt ticket sales. The play's popularity inspired publishers to bring out a second edition of *Frankenstein* in 1823 (the first on which Mary Shelley's name appeared). *Presumption*, which traveled to theaters in the English provinces, also traveled across the Atlantic where audiences saw the play in 1825 at New York's Park Theatre. Unlike the London production, which had excited protest, the American version received, in the words of the *New York Evening Post*, "the most unbounded applause."[44] American audiences were less familiar with the scandalous Percy Shelley circle which may explain why they did not find the play as objectionable as their British counterparts. Over the next twenty years, producers in both America and Europe reprised the play several times.

Peake was not the only playwright to adapt the Frankenstein story for the stage. Within three years of the first performance of *Presumption*, fourteen other dramatizations of *Frankenstein* appeared on English and French stages. Versions of *Frankenstein* were especially popular in France, where the monster came to personify mob rule and violence. This association of the monster with radical politics and social upheaval persisted over the course of the nineteenth century in both England and France.

Scene from *Frankenstein; or, The Model Man*
Photographic reproduction of a contemporary English wood engraving
Courtesy The Granger Collection, New York

By the mid-nineteenth century, the popular Frankenstein melodrama had become a subject for parody. The 1850 production of *The Model Man,* for example, burlesqued the consistent blue complexion of the stage monster by having Dr. Frankenstein sing:

I've put him together with joint & screw
And to finish him off with a touch or two
Of red just here—and a tinge of blue
And I don't mind saying I think he'll do.

T.P. Cooke as the monster in *Presumption; or, The Fate of Frankenstein*
Nathaniel Whittock (fl. 1829–1848)
Lithograph
Courtesy The Harvard Theatre Collection, The Houghton Library

English actor Thomas Potter Cooke played the monster wearing blue body paint, greenish face make-up, and black painted lips. Cooke's portrayal of the monster was to the nineteenth century what Boris Karloff would become in the twentieth century, namely the dominant visual image of the monster.

As early as the 1820s, the name "Frankenstein" became a rhetorical tool used by some English legislators to delay liberalizing reforms. Speaking against the emancipation of slaves in the West Indies in 1824, one year after the first stage productions of *Frankenstein,* the British Foreign Secretary George Canning observed of the slave, "To turn him loose in the manhood of his physical strength, in the maturity of his physical passion, but in the infancy of his uninstructed reason, would be to raise up a creature resembling the splendid fiction of a recent romance."[45] In comparing the slave to a monster out of control, Canning did not confuse the monster with his creator Victor Frankenstein, but others quickly did so. English novelist Elizabeth Gaskell made the identification

THE IRISH FRANKENSTEIN.

The Irish Frankenstein
Artist unknown
Photographic reproduction of an illustration
appearing in *Punch,* 1843
*Courtesy Library of Congress, Prints and
Photographs Division*

By the 1840s, the name Frankenstein and the
concept of the monster had become fused in
the popular imagination. In this early cartoon,
an Irish "monster" (note the horns and the
man's massive stature) menaces an English
gentleman with a shillelagh.

THE BRUMMAGEM FRANKENSTEIN.

The Brummagem Frankenstein
John Tenniel
Photographic reproduction of an illustration appearing in *Punch,* 1866
Courtesy Pennsylvania State University Libraries

British illustrator Sir John Tenniel produced more than two thousand cartoons for the popular journal *Punch,* as well as illustrations for Lewis Carroll's *Alice in Wonderland.* In this cartoon, the politically conservative Tenniel cast the working man as a Frankenstein monster. The hulking working man waits to be granted the right to vote from liberal members of Parliament with the predictable bad results (so Tenniel implies).

of the monster as Frankenstein explicit in her 1848 novel *Mary Barton:* "The actions of the uneducated seem to me typified in those of Frankenstein, that monster of many human qualities, ungifted with soul, a knowledge of good and evil."[46]

In the second half of the nineteenth century, British artists employed the Frankenstein monster in their political satires. In several cartoons for the popular British magazine *Punch*, artist John Tenniel (better known today as the illustrator for Lewis Carroll's *Alice in Wonderland)* used the image of the Frankenstein monster to make a political point. In 1866 he depicted the working class as monstrous in his cartoon "The Brummagem Frankenstein."[47] (Brummagem comes from the vernacular pronounciation for the English city of Birmingham, where much cheap jewelry and gilt toys were manufactured.) The enormous working man, massive in size like the Frankenstein monster, waits for the vote to be given to him by liberal members of Parliament. The danger, the cartoonist implied, is the potential for such a monster to run amok once he possesses voting rights. In 1882 Tenniel cast Irish nationalist leader Charles Stewart Parnell as the "Irish Frankenstein."[48] The Irish, like the working class, were considered by the English to be brutish and primitive and, like a monster, possessing the potential to run out of control.[49] Across the Atlantic in the United States, political allusions to Frankenstein similarly appeared. Massachusetts Senator Charles Sumner, a notable advocate for the emancipation of slaves, reportedly compared the Southern Confederacy to the "soulless monster of Frankenstein, the wretched creation of mortal science without God."[50]

Over the course of the nineteenth century identifying the monster and not the scientist as Frankenstein, begun in the 1820s, continued steadily. Maintained in fiction, the popular press, and on the stage, this Frankenstein had already been stripped of many of the qualities that Mary Shelley gave him. Reduced in his ability to speak, the monster retained his massive size and his potential for destruction. Most of the nineteenth-century allusions to Frankenstein were political in nature. The working class, the uneducated, and the Irish all received the "Frankenstein" label, illustrating middle and upper class fears about these groups. As novelist Joseph Conrad noted, "fashions in monsters do change." In

THE RUSSIAN FRANKENSTEIN AND HIS MONSTER.

The Russian Frankenstein and His Monster
Artist unknown
Photographic reproduction of an illustration appearing in *Punch,* 1854
Courtesy Pennsylvania State University Libraries

During the Crimean War, British enemy Tsar Nicholas I was depicted as the Russian Frankenstein who, after creating a militarist monster, allows it to run amok.

Frankenstein
Edison Manufacturing Company, 1910
Photographic reproduction of movie frames
Courtesy Library of Congress, Motion Pictures Division

In these film stills, Dr. Frankenstein (Augustus Philips) and his fiancée (Mary Fuller) are interrupted by the monster he created in his laboratory. In a fury, the creature kills the young woman beloved by Frankenstein.

the twentieth century, the Frankenstein myth would undergo another transformation. Amid the increasing cultural relevance of science in American society, the Frankenstein monster, aided by the powerful new medium of film, would become a potent symbol of scientific ambition gone astray.

HOLLYWOOD PRODUCES *FRANKENSTEIN*

In the early twentieth century, film offered another avenue for cultural penetration of the Frankenstein tale. In 1910 the Edison Manufacturing Company released a fifteen-minute, silent version of Mary Shelley's *Frankenstein*. The film, directed by J. Searle Dawley and featuring Charles Stanton Ogle in white make-up as the monster, presented the formation of the monster from chemicals boiling in a huge cauldron in Victor Frankenstein's laboratory, rather than from the electrical apparatus that would dominate later interpretations of the monster's genesis.[51] In adapting the story for the screen, the Edison Company strove "to eliminate all the actually repulsive situations and to concentrate its endeavors upon the mystic and psychological problems" of Shelley's tale. Bad reviews, however, prompted the company to withdraw the film from circulation.[52]

Stage productions of *Frankenstein* continued in the twentieth century. A 1915 theater production *The Last Laugh* was one of the first adaptations to use electricity to animate the dead flesh of the creature. In the play, the monster is brought to life by the application of electrical current to a band of iron around his feet.[53] "The scenic effects of the play are impressively realistic" noted one critic in praise of the laboratory scenes, "in fact, the operating room, with its electrical machines buzzing, the oxygen and apparatus around give the average layman the creeps." By featuring contemporary science and medicine, the play's producers updated the Frankenstein story, making it accessible to a new generation of theater-goers.

In 1927 a new version of the Frankenstein story for the stage would provide the basis for the 1931 Universal film containing the visual image of the Frankenstein monster that would come to dominate the twentieth century. Peggy Webling's *Frankenstein: An Adventure in the Macabre* premiered in London

The EDISON KINETOGRAM

VOL. 2   MARCH 15, 1910   No. 4

SCENE FROM

FRANKENSTEIN

FILM No. 6604

EDISON FILMS RELEASED FROM MARCH 16 TO 31 INCLUSIVE

The Edison Kinetogram, March 15,1910
Photographic reproduction of a journal
Courtesy U.S. Department of the Interior, National Park Service, Edison National Historic Site

Charles Stanton Ogle, in dramatic white make-up, played the first screen Frankenstein monster.

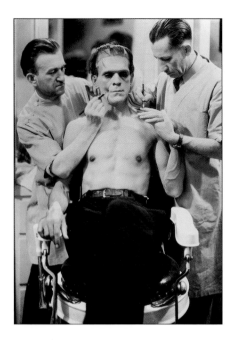

Jack Pierce and his assistant make up Boris Karloff as the Frankenstein monster
Courtesy Museum of Modern Art, Film Stills Archive
Reproduced courtesy Universal Studios Licensing, Inc.

According to actress Elsa Lanchester who played the role of the Frankenstein monster's bride, make-up artist Jack Pierce took his creative responsibilities very seriously, wearing a doctor's operating gown when he prepared actors' make-up for the Frankenstein films. Pierce studied human anatomy and surgical technique to create the visually distinctive look of both the monster and his mate.

Frankenstein
Edison Films, 1910
Photographic reproduction of a movie frame
Courtesy Library of Congress, Motion Pictures Division

The first cinematic *Frankenstein* was a silent film with a running time of fifteen minutes. In the film, the monster arises from a vat of chemicals, rather than reanimating in response to electrical stimuli.

and featured actor Hamilton Deane as the creature. Deane's success in the stage version of *Dracula* (the story of an aristocratic vampire) both in London and New York helped persuade film producers at Universal Studios that American audiences would attend "horror films." In 1930 Universal Studios purchased film rights for Webling's play and its adaptation by John Balderston for $20,000. Directed by James Whale and introducing obscure actor Boris Karloff as the monster, Universal released *Frankenstein* to rave reviews. The movie proved immensely successful for the studio: produced for $290,000, it earned more than $12 million.[54] *The New York Times* named *Frankenstein*, along with *Arrowsmith* and *A Connecticut Yankee*, one of the top ten films of the year.[55] Success with the film inspired the studio to release several sequels, as well as a host of imitations.[56]

When Universal acquired Webling's story, the producers made several significant changes. Screenwriter John Russell introduces the plot device of using a criminal brain rather than a normal brain in order to explain the monster's urge to kill.[57] Whereas in Shelley's novel the monster reverts to murder only after enduring abuse from the humans he encounters, the Universal film emphasizes that the monster's evil results from his criminal brain. In the film, a professor lectures his students on cranial anatomy, and locates the depravity of a criminal in the malformations of his brain: "These degenerate characteristics," Professor Waldman informs his class, "check amazingly with the case history of the dead man before us, whose life was one of brutality, of violence, and of murder."[58]

After Henry Frankenstein's laboratory assistant accidentally drops the normal brain, he brings the criminal brain to his master, who unwittingly transplants it into the monster. Biology becomes destiny. (Why producers changed Victor Frankenstein's name to Henry remains a mystery.) Unlike Mary Shelley's novel in which Victor dies and the monster disappears, the 1931 film ends with serious injury for the scientist and the death of the monster, heavily symbolic of the penalty for transgressing natural law. Of course, given the success of the original, Universal producers had no qualms about resurrecting the monster for the 1935 sequel *The Bride of Frankenstein*.

Audiences were deeply affected by the film, for which studio publicity agents, seeking to intensify the experience, arranged to have nurses on duty in the theaters, free "tonics" for the nervous, and the firing of a gun backstage to startle theater patrons.[59] Mordaunt Hall, film critic for *The New York Times*, noted that the "morbid, gruesome affair" aroused so much excitement at the theater "that many in the audience laughed to cover their true feeling."[60] Even before the film's release, Universal producers had received warnings from the censors at the Motion Picture Production Code Administration (known as the Hays Office) about the horrific potential of many of the scenes and urged care in depicting such events as showing a hanged man from whom body parts would be salvaged. Abroad, the film generated criticism for "undue gruesomeness" and "an alleged irreverent attitude on the part of some of the characters, particularly whenever they suggested that their actions were paralleling those of the Creator."[61] Several

Poster for *Frankenstein*, 1931
Photographic reproduction of a poster
Courtesy The Granger Collection, New York

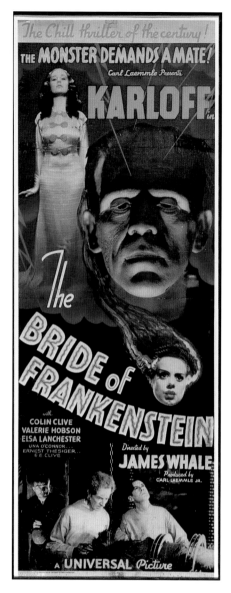

Poster for *The Bride of Frankenstein*, 1935
Photographic reproduction of a poster
Courtesy The Granger Collection, New York

In the 1935 sequel, actress Elsa Lanchester played both Mary Shelley and the monster's mate. Lanchester's striking, streaked hair and make-up have made her image, like that of Karloff, recognizable to millions in the years since the film's release.

Poster for the double feature *Son of Frankenstein* and *The Bride of Frankenstein*
Photographic reproduction of a poster
Courtesy © Bettmann/CORBIS

In both sequels to the 1931 film, Universal filmmakers appropriated actual scientific devices for use in their productions. *The Bride of Frankenstein*, for example, included the first electric pacemaker to appear in popular film. The doctor used the device to maintain the heart of a murdered woman before he transplanted the organ into the monster's bride. In *Son of Frankenstein*, the monster undergoes fluoroscopy, a technology in which x-rays, after passing through the interior of the body, are projected onto a fluorescent screen. Although fluoroscopy had been introduced in the early twentieth century, the technology was greatly enhanced by improvements in the 1930s and 1940s.

countries (Sweden, Italy, Northern Ireland) banned the film altogether. Such problems recurred in sequels to *Frankenstein* until the 1960s.

The enduring visual impact of the Frankenstein monster in the 1931 production and in subsequent Universal films (such as *The Bride of Frankenstein* [1935] and *Son of Frankenstein* [1939]) owed much to the skill of make-up artist Jack Pierce who turned Boris Karloff into the monster recognized everywhere

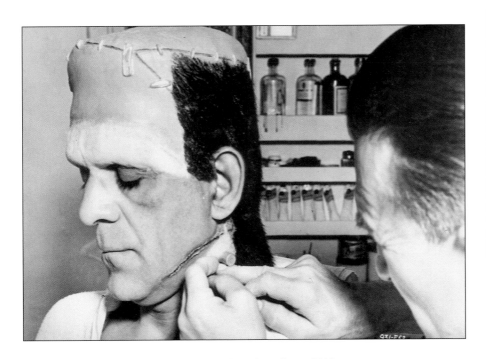

Jack Pierce makes up Boris Karloff for *Son of Frankenstein,* ca. 1939
Courtesy Photofest
Reproduced courtesy Universal Studios Licensing, Inc.

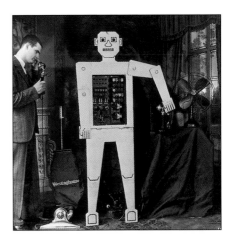

Westinghouse Laboratories's mechanical man *Televox,* 1928
Courtesy Westinghouse Electric Corporation

One inspiration for the 1931 Frankenstein monster was the mechanical man developed in 1927 at the Westinghouse Electric Corporation in Pittsburgh, Pennsylvania. Although the Frankenstein monster is created from human flesh, he moved with a characteristically stilted, almost mechanical walk. Karloff wore a five-pound metal rod under his shirt to produce the effect.

today. Pierce developed the idea of creating a human monster, distorted by the efforts of his creator to make a man. He credited science for the way he designed the monster's make-up. "In 1931," he told reporters from *The New York Times*, "I spent three months of research in anatomy, surgery, medicine, criminal history, criminology, ancient and modern burial customs, and electrodynamics." From his anatomical studies, Pierce reasoned that a practical surgeon would place a human brain in the skull in the simplest way. He would cut "the top of the skull off straight across like a pot lid, hinge it, pop the brain in and then clamp it on tight."[62] Pierce's reasoning inspired the square, flat head associated with Karloff's monster.

The two metal studs protruding from the monster's neck also originated with Pierce. Although often mistaken for bolts, the studs were actually inlets for electricity, "plugs such as we use for our lamps or flatirons."[63] To produce the

monster's stilted walk, Pierce also designed a five-pound metal spine (the rod carrying current to the creature's brain) which the audience did not see.[64] Pierce and director James Whale drew inspiration from technological developments in the 1920s and the "machine-age aesthetic" then dominant in the arts. One of their sources may have been Westinghouse Laboratories, which in 1927 introduced *Televox,* an automaton with a square head and metal arms and legs attached by bolts.[65] Televox did not speak, but he could wave his arms, lift a telephone receiver, and operate switches to control machines. "Although there has been much speculation about these so-called 'robots,' by newspaper writers and readers," one Westinghouse engineer observed, "we have constructed them principally as a dramatic way of illustrating methods of electrical control."[66]

BOUNDARY CROSSINGS IN 1931

The 1930s, like Shelley's time, were rife with speculation about the origins of life and the boundary between life and death. Reviving the dead generated intense popular interest, as did efforts to achieve "immortality" through the use of organ transplants, artificial organs, and other devices.[67]

In 1934 newspapers around the country reported sensational experiments in which a University of California biochemist successfully revived a dog asphyxiated with nitrogen gas. Photographs of Robert E. Cornish and his dog, Lazarus IV, appeared in *Newsweek,* the *Literary Digest,* and *Popular Science Monthly.* Reporters closely monitored the dog's progress; interviews with prominent scientists fanned speculation about restoring the dead. The successful "revival" of dogs like Lazarus IV was marred by concern that the process altered the animal's mental state. "The fear that such experimentation on a human being would evolve a fiendish Frankenstein monster," noted a reporter, prevented Cornish from accepting "offers by scores of persons to sacrifice themselves to death as a test of man's power over life."[69] Although Cornish did not accept such offers, he did seek permission to attempt his technique on men executed in the gas chambers of Arizona, Colorado, and Nevada.[70] His failure to gain access to prisoners for such efforts did not detract from ongoing speculation about the boundary between life and death.

After 1935 newspapers and magazines devoted considerable coverage to the "glass heart" developed by the team of aviator Charles Lindbergh and eminent French surgeon Alexis Carrel. The Nobel Prize-winning Carrel, known for his work on animal kidney transplants at the Rockefeller Institute for Medical Research, worked with Lindbergh to develop a device to aid the aviator's sister-in-law, who suffered from a serious heart disease.[71] Together they devised a perfusion pump made of Pyrex glass, which would maintain organs removed from the body for study or for transplantation back into the animal.[72] By 1935 they had sustained a variety of animal organs (hearts, kidneys, ovaries, spleens, adrenal glands) connected to their pump in a germ-free glass tank.[73]

American newspapers also reported that physicians in Russia had achieved some success in experiments that used a simple pump, operated by an electric motor, to send oxygenated blood through the arteries in a rhythmic pulse. Connecting the pump to the arteries and veins of a suicide three hours dead, the physicians "revived" the man for two minutes; he reportedly opened his eyes and appeared to look at the doctors.[74]

Newspapers similarly covered the development of artificial pacemakers and other electrical devices that affected the heart rhythm. New York cardiologist Albert Hyman constructed a device to resuscitate the stopped heart and to treat heart-block and other serious arrhythmias.[75] Sensational accounts of Hyman's experiments, however, created some difficulties for the physician; he endured "abusive correspondence, and even lawsuits from irascible people who regarded his resuscitation endeavors as sacrilegious tampering with Divine Providence."[76]

That filmmakers responded to public discussions about innovations in cardiac and resuscitation research is evident in a number of films released in the 1930s. The Universal Frankenstein films, for example, featured electrical resuscitation devices. *The Bride of Frankenstein* was the first motion picture to depict a cardiac pacemaker.[77] In the film, the pacemaker is used to maintain the heart of

Perfusion pump
Photograph courtesy Rockefeller University Archives

Aviator Charles Lindbergh, working closely with surgeon Alexis Carrel, developed a "glass heart," a perfusion pump that maintained organs removed from the body.

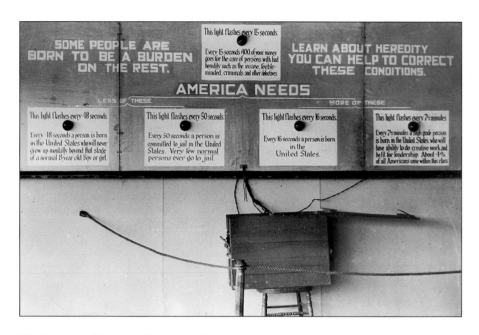

Display from a "Fitter Families Contest"
Courtesy American Philosophical Society, Philadelphia

American eugenicists used this display with its flashing lights at many state fairs around the United States, emphasizing some of the economic arguments in favor of eugenics and eugenic sterilization.

a murdered woman in a fluid-filled jar until the organ can be placed into the body of the "bride." Some people have speculated that the appearance of such devices in "macabre" films like *Frankenstein* may have derailed the development of the pacemaker and other technologies by creating the public criticism that Albert Hyman encountered.[78]

Mary Shelley, who ascribed the creature's crimes to his alienation from human society, would have been surprised to learn that the monster in the 1931 film was evil because he had received a criminal brain. Such biological determinism, however, was popular among Americans in the early decades of the twentieth century. Many people considered heredity rather than environment, economic system, or education to be the critical factor in problems of social unrest, immigration, unemployment, and crime. These people looked to the sci-

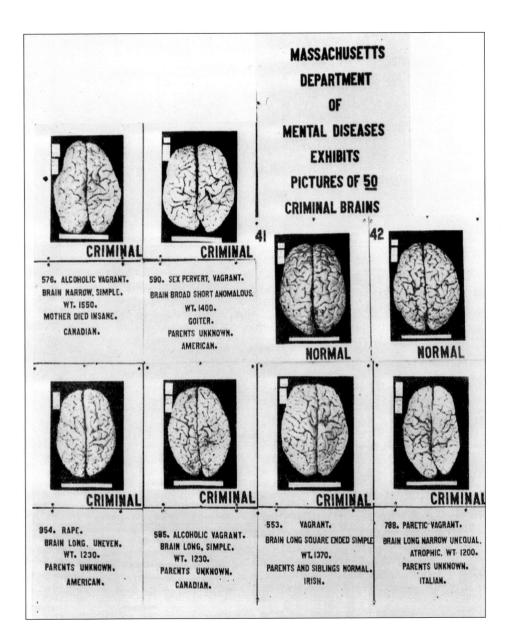

MASSACHUSETTS
DEPARTMENT
OF
MENTAL DISEASES
EXHIBITS
PICTURES OF 50
CRIMINAL BRAINS

CRIMINAL

576. ALCOHOLIC VAGRANT.
BRAIN NARROW, SIMPLE.
WT. 1550.
MOTHER DIED INSANE.
CANADIAN.

CRIMINAL

590. SEX PERVERT, VAGRANT.
BRAIN BROAD SHORT ANOMALOUS.
WT. 1400.
GOITER.
PARENTS UNKNOWN.
AMERICAN.

NORMAL

NORMAL

CRIMINAL

954. RAPE.
BRAIN LONG, UNEVEN.
WT. 1230.
PARENTS UNKNOWN.
AMERICAN.

CRIMINAL

585. ALCOHOLIC VAGRANT.
BRAIN LONG, SIMPLE.
WT. 1230.
PARENTS UNKNOWN.
CANADIAN.

CRIMINAL

553. VAGRANT.
BRAIN LONG SQUARE ENDED SIMPLE
WT. 1370.
PARENTS AND SIBLINGS NORMAL.
IRISH.

CRIMINAL

788. PARETIC VAGRANT.
BRAIN LONG NARROW UNEQUAL.
ATROPHIC, WT. 1200.
PARENTS UNKNOWN.
ITALIAN.

The Brains of Criminals
Photographic reproduction of an illustration from Harry H. Laughlin, *The Second International Exhibition of Eugenics,* 1923
Courtesy Pennsylvania State University Libraries

Displayed at the Second International Exhibition of Eugenics held in 1921 at the American Museum of Natural History in New York City, these photographs supposedly demonstrated the physical differences between normal and criminal brains. In the 1931 Universal film, the murderous behavior of the Frankenstein monster results when he receives a criminal brain.

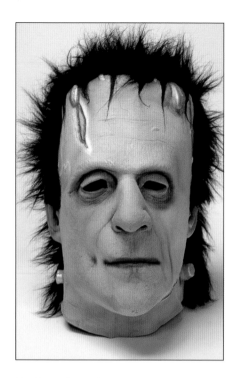

Frankenstein mask, 1995
Courtesy The Bakken

ence of eugenics to promote the reproduction of those with a sound genetic background and to prevent those who did not. Fearing that the "wrong people" would reproduce, a number of American states adopted compulsory sterilization laws for criminals, mentally retarded adults, epileptics, and other institutionalized individuals to insure that these populations would not breed.

In 1927, the United States Supreme Court upheld the constitutionality of compulsory sterilization in the *Buck* v. *Bell* decision in which Justice Oliver Wendell Holmes pronounced "three generations of imbeciles are enough."[79] By 1937 a *Fortune* magazine survey reported that more than two-thirds of its readers approved the sterilization of mental defectives, and some 63 percent favored the sterilization of criminals.[80] Director James Whale and his production team exploited such biological determinism when they created a monster whose evil results from the lobes of his brain rather than his experiences or character.

FEATURE CREATURE

The image of the Frankenstein monster is immediately recognizable today in consumer products, cartoons, newspaper headlines, and other media. How should we understand the enormous popularity of *Frankenstein* and its many interpretations? Part of the answer lies in the very elasticity of the story (a scientist creates a monster who runs out of control) and its ability to support multiple, even conflicting, interpretations. Much of the durability of the Frankenstein myth in the twentieth century reflects the enormous power of screen images to concentrate collective experiences and images in the minds of mass audiences.

The nature of film and movie spectatorship have contributed to the perpetuation of the Frankenstein myth. Isolated in the darkness of the movie theater, viewers experienced a personal version of the film as they simultaneously shared the culture that produced popular movies. "For the Frankenstein myth, film itself is evidence of Mary Shelley's prophecy come true—the culmination of what Professor Waldman called the power 'to mock the invisible world with its own shadows.' Alone together at the movies, we experience the fusion of self, society and technology that is the domain of the myth of Frankenstein."[81]

Frankenstein gum cards, ca. 1960s
Courtesy Toy Scouts, Inc., Akron, Ohio
Reproduced courtesy Universal Studios Licensing, Inc.

The creature that inspired disgust and horror has continued to appear in films and in other media. In 1957, the film *I Was a Teenage Frankenstein*, in which Professor Frankenstein makes a monster from the bodies of teenage victims of a car wreck, appealed to adolescent audiences. The same year Britain's Hammer Studios initiated a new cycle of Frankenstein films, much gorier and graphic than the earlier Universal series.[82] In 1994 filmmaker Kenneth Branagh directed *Mary Shelley's Frankenstein*, claiming to recover the original story Shelley had intended. Thus, the Frankenstein myth remains a story that can be reworked for each generation of filmgoers.

Horror movies, an enduring feature of twentieth-century American culture since the 1930s, have served to displace fears about tumultuous social and economic changes in these decades. In the 1930s and 1940s, for example, screen horrors of *Frankenstein*, *Dracula*, and others attracted audiences disheartened by the Great Depression and the fear of world war. In the 1950s and 1960s fears and anxieties provoked by the specter of nuclear holocaust and the harsh rhetoric and reality of the Cold War brought audiences to theaters in which atomic monsters roamed the earth.[83]

The Frankenstein films and their visual impact have in turn influenced other genres of mass culture. Beginning with the Universal films, movies based on the Frankenstein story spurred the reissue of Mary Shelley's novel, which,

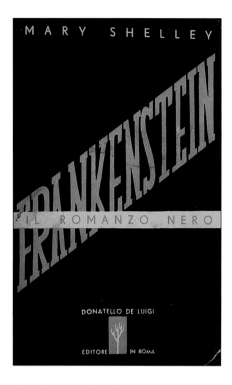

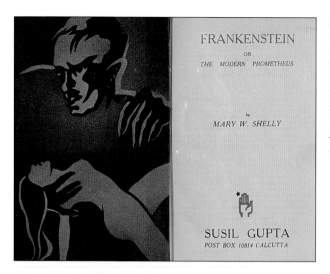

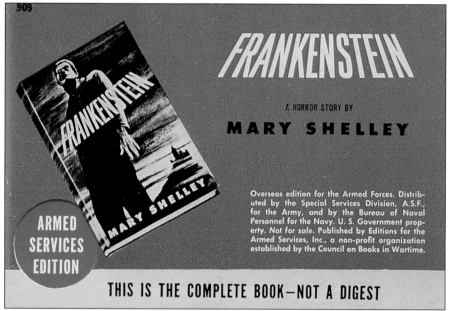

Mary Shelley (1797–1851)
Frankenstein
Donatello de Luigi, Rome, 1944
Courtesy The Carl H. Pforzheimer Collection of Shelley and His Circle, The New York Public Library, Astor, Lenox and Tilden Foundations

Mary Shelley (1797–1851)
Frankenstein or the Modern Promethus
Susil Gupta, Calcutta, 1944
Courtesy The Carl H. Pforzheimer Collection of Shelley and His Circle, The New York Public Library, Astor, Lenox and Tilden Foundations

Poster for The Armed Forces Edition for *Frankenstein*
Photographic reproduction of a poster
Courtesy Harry Ransom Humanities Research Center, The University of Texas at Austin

Mary Shelley's complex *Frankenstein,* never out of print since 1823, continues to exist alongside the mass culture Frankenstein monster. Following the success of the Universal Studios *Frankenstein* series of the 1930s, Shelley's novel appeared in an Armed Services Edition for American servicemen and women during World War II.

Frankenstein All Plastic Assembly Kit (left)
Courtesy Toy Scouts, Inc., Akron, Ohio

Frankenstein wind-up toy, 1995 (center)
Courtesy The Bakken
Reproduced courtesy Universal Studios Licensing, Inc.

Official Universal Studio Monsters: Frankenstein, 1991 (right)
Courtesy Susan E. Lederer
Reproduced courtesy Universal Studios Licensing, Inc.

since 1818, has been available in a great variety of editions. The first American edition of *Frankenstein*, a reprint of the two-volume 1823 edition, was published in Philadelphia in 1833. Between 1865 and 1942, American publishers issued some nineteen editions of the original 1818 text, including a digest-size "Armed Services Edition" of *Frankenstein* available to American servicemen during World War II. The 1831 edition of Shelley's novel, which contained the new introduction and several revisions, received similar attention from American publishers. Publishers produced the book in cheap paperback versions, in leather-bound illustrated editions, in comic-book form, and as a serial in magazines like *Weird Tales*. In 1960 the National Library Service for the Blind and Physically

An advertisement for plastic model kits made by Aurora, ca. 1962
Courtesy Boy Scouts of America, Irving, Texas
Reproduced courtesy Universal Studios Licensing, Inc.

In the early 1960s monster kits "frightfully easy to assemble" offered adolescents the opportunity to surprise their mothers and demonstrated the appeal of monster culture.

Handicapped issued a Braille edition for visually-impaired readers.[84] Today the novel is accessible on the Internet. Thus, the Frankenstein monster of twentieth-century popular culture exists along side the very different, if lesser known, monster of Mary Shelley's original.

Over the years Frankenstein toys and games, breakfast cereals, plastic model kits, coloring books, and Halloween costumes feature yet another facet of the Frankenstein monster. In adapting the monster for children's consumption, the horror of a creature constructed from body parts and tissue stolen from graves becomes somewhat muted, as do his murderous crimes. Nonetheless, the monster remains a source of menace, a creature out of control, and a product of science. Toys and games featuring the Frankenstein monster allow children the opportunity to experience in a more controlled way the frisson of horror about dead bodies returning to life, wreaking havoc and destruction. Cartoons in the 1930s and 1940s in which such characters as Betty Boop and Mighty Mouse encountered a child's version of the Frankenstein monster helped to insure that the monster would live on in popular culture.

In the 1960s, perhaps the heyday of "monster culture," movie-monster model kits competed with plastic model kits of fighter planes and ships for the dollars of adolescent boys. Introduced by Aurora Plastics, advertisements for the model kits "laboratory-tested hobby kits for the boy who has everything" emphasized both American affluence and the enduring adolescent appeal of "surprising your mother." During the 1960s, amid the political tensions of the Cuban missile crisis, monsters, as cultural historian David Skal has noted, "provided elements of reassurance." Creatures like Frankenstein and Dracula, who defied death, offered "an image of survival, however distorted or grotesque."[85]

In a lighter vein, television producers in the 1960s also mined the Frankenstein myth for entertainment. Perhaps in light of the intimacy of watching television in one's own home, the monster became thoroughly domesticated in the popular comedy *The Munsters*. By 1974 the conventions of the Frankenstein horror film had become so ritualized and familiar they could be parodied, as in Mel Brooks's production *Young Frankenstein*.[86]

In the late twentieth century, the Frankenstein monster remains a vibrant element of cultural literacy, immediately recognizable in film and television, in

Margaret Thatcher as Lady Frankenstein
Artist unknown
Photographic reproduction of an illustration appearing in *Punch,* November 28, 1990
Courtesy Pennsylvania State University Libraries
Reproduced by permission of Punch Ltd.

Here Frankenstein appears as a political metaphor. In this case, a female Frankenstein monster (former British Prime Minister Margaret Thatcher) creates a monstrous Conservative party.

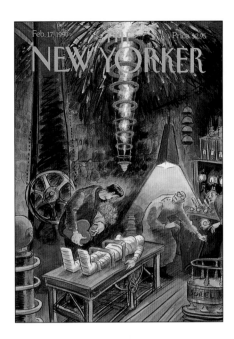

Ghouls Rush In
The New Yorker
February 17, 1997
Edward Sorel
Cover drawing by Edward Sorel; ©1997
The New Yorker Magazine, Inc.

The Frankenstein monster remains a vibrant element of cultural literacy.

Gary Larson cartoons, and on the covers of *The New Yorker.* This recognition reflects both the power of the movies to fix images in the collective consciousness (it is the Karloff monster with the distinctive flat head and massive size that people recognize) and the shared knowledge of the essential elements of the Frankenstein myth (a monster out of control, transgressive science).[87] *Frankenstein,* in addition to being a distinctive visual image, endures as a potent metaphor for certain societal anxieties. In newspaper headlines, magazine articles, and television stories, the Frankenstein monster remains an element of the American cultural vocabulary, a means to express fears and anxieties about the implications of new developments in science and medicine.

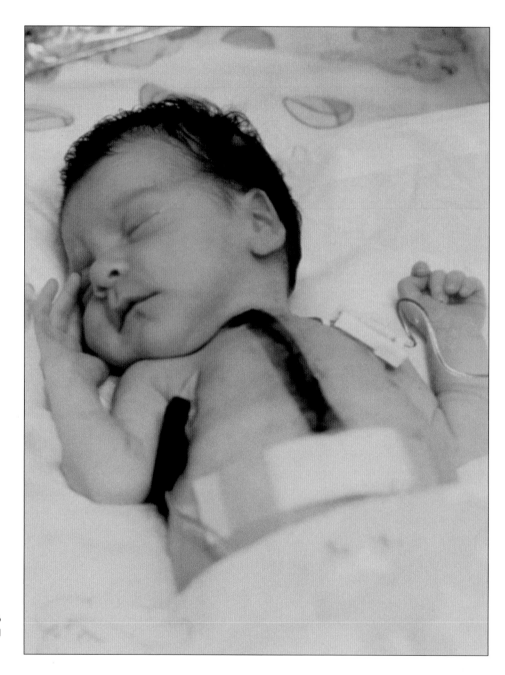

Baby Fae, October 30, 1984
Courtesy © Bettmann/CORBIS

In 1984 Baby Fae became the first infant to
receive a baboon heart transplant. She survived
for little over a month with the animal organ.

PROMISE AND PERIL

In the late twentieth century, the pace of scientific progress increases, as does our concern about society's ability to retain control of the dazzling new technologies that are currently shaping our understanding of what it means to be human. Frankenstein—man, monster, myth, and metaphor—has offered and continues to offer a means to articulate uneasiness about the future, and the story has been invoked in response to an array of scientific innovations. Over the course of the twentieth century, the atomic bomb, organ transplants, xenografting (the use of animal organs in human bodies), genetic engineering, in vitro fertilization, and most recently, cloning have all provoked comparisons to the Frankenstein myth. Amid the furor, for example, over recombinant DNA research in the 1970s, the mayor of Cambridge, Massachusetts, who opposed a DNA laboratory at Harvard, invoked the Frankenstein comparison to make his point: "They may come up with a disease that can't be cured, even a monster. Is this the answer to Dr. Frankenstein's dream?"[88] These Frankenstein allusions offer a vocabulary to discuss the social and policy questions that society raises in the context of scientific change.

In the face of new medical and scientific developments come several questions: how can we as a society successfully negotiate the limits of acceptable science? How can we balance the interests of individuals confronting life-threatening illnesses with the need to protect society from the threat of disease? How can we make informed decisions about scientific advances that seem to be happening all at once and all around us? Although there are no easy answers to these questions, the history of medicine offers some lessons about the ways in which experts and lay people have resolved these issues.

The Cow Pock-or-the-Wonderful Effects of the New Inoculation!
James Gillray (1757–1815)
Photographic reproduction of an etching appearing in *Vide—the Publications of ye Anti-Vaccine Society,* June 12, 1802

British caricaturist James Gillray lampooned the effects of physician Edward Jenner's new cowpox vaccine. The cow heads sprouting up on patients' bodies suggest fears about the violation of natural boundaries between animals and humans.

THE SEARCH FOR BALANCE

In Mary Shelley's day, the introduction of smallpox vaccination (first performed by English physician Edward Jenner in 1796) raised profoundly disturbing questions about the "unnaturalness" and uncertainty of intentionally introducing diseased animal matter (cowpox) into the human blood stream.[89] Vaccinators like Jenner who used cowpox as the source of vaccine to protect patients from the deadly smallpox experienced both hostility and derision. In the nineteenth century organized anti-vaccination societies worked to repeal compulsory smallpox vaccination statutes and to establish that vaccination was a threat to both public and personal health rather than a benefit. Less than one hundred years later, smallpox no longer threatened most Americans. After an unprecedented international vaccination effort spearheaded by the World Health Organization (WHO), public health experts and researchers eradicated smallpox in 1980 around the world. In 1996 WHO's governing body called for the destruction of the two known virus stocks held under tight security at the Centers for Disease Control in Atlanta and at the Vector Institute in Siberia. WHO has scheduled the destruction of the virus in 2002, although concern about the potential threat of smallpox as a bioweapon is likely to delay these plans.[90]

Recent advances in immunology and genetics raise the possibility that animal organs may soon be successfully used for transplantation into human beings. Although scientists have thus far attempted xenografting or xenotransplantation (the use of organs and tissue between different species) in only a few human patients, the process offers the hope that lives of sick people in desperate need of organ transplants can be saved. Some scientists have questioned the safety of such transplants, given the uncertain risks associated with the procedures. Primate virologist Jonathan Allen, for example, insists that using baboon tissue in humans at this stage is dangerous in light of recent experience with emerging viruses and the potential for transmitting new animal viruses to humans. "Once the door is open and a new virus is unleashed," Allan argues, "it will be a monumental task to identify a new pathogen, develop adequate screening tests and prevent the spread of that new infection."[91] Other people express moral objections to the use of animal organs. "To some," notes Joseph Palca, a science correspondent for National Public Radio, "it seems dangerously close to 'playing God.'"[92]

In the 1980s the possibility that animals could be used as a source of organs for desperately ill human recipients repulsed some individuals. When the infant identified in the media as Baby Fae received a baboon heart at Loma Linda Medical Center in 1984, some critics attacked the experiment as unnatural, unwarranted, and unsupported by medical evidence.[93] Advances in drugs to suppress the immune system, as well as genetics, have prompted renewed experi-

Jeff Getty, 1996
Courtesy Lou Damatteis/Reuters/Getty Images

In January 1996 AIDS patient Jeff Getty left San Francisco General Hospital after receiving a baboon bone-marrow transplant.

mentation with xenografts in the 1990s. In 1992 Los Angeles doctors transplanted the liver from a pig into a woman dying of hepatitis. In 1995, with permission from the Food and Drug Administration, patients with advanced Parkinson's disease received injections of fetal pig brain cells. In a much publicized case in 1996, Jeff Getty, an AIDS patient in San Francisco, received baboon bone marrow in the hope that this would enhance his damaged immune system.[94] Medical researchers continue to follow Getty's progress in an ongoing effort to determine the value of such experimental therapies in alleviating diseases like AIDS. It remains uncertain how valuable these experimental therapies will be in achieving the goal of reducing human disease.

The possibility of large-scale use of genetically-altered animal kidneys, livers, marrow, and hearts to redress the desperate shortage of human organs for transplantation renews old questions about proceeding in the face of the unknown. How do we balance the potential risks and potential benefits? How does xenografting affect, if at all, our understanding of what it means to be human and our relationships to the animal world? "Even if people aren't overly concerned about farming pigs," the journal *Science* noted in 1994, "medical ethicists worry that they will find the use of pig or baboon organs too 'unnatural' to be acceptable for human transplantation."[95] A 1998 survey conducted by the National Kidney Foundation suggests that many Americans accept the concept of xenotransplantation as a viable option. In a poll of 1,200 randomly selected Americans, nearly 75 percent surveyed reported that they would consider a xenotransplant for a loved one if an organ or tissue were not available from a human donor.[96]

The Food and Drug Administration and other governmental agencies have held several public meetings to address the scientific, legal, and ethical issues associated with cross-species transplants. In July 1999 the Secretary of Health and Human Services chartered a Secretary's Advisory Committee on Xenotransplantation to consider the scientific, medical, social, and ethical issues arising from cross-species transplants. This committee and other associated committees hold ongoing public meetings to obtain public input into the development of policies for the regulations of xenotransplantation.[97] At this stage, no one can safely predict whether xenotransplantation will be a tremendous boon to

The University of California, San Diego, teaches anatomy to medical students in part through the Anatomic VisualizeR©, a computer program that lets students "dissect" virtual anatomical models of various organs. The models are derived from the National Library of Medicine's Visible Human Male.

medical progress, and like vaccination, a means to eradicate diseases that plague humankind, or whether it will be a medical dead end, abandoned after false starts and failures.

VIRTUAL ANATOMY

Although xenografting remains an uncertain procedure, the history of anatomical dissection offers an illustration of the ways in which physicians and laypeople have successfully resolved the conflict between the needs of medical progress and social values. In Shelley's day and through the early twentieth century, the idea of cutting into bodies of the dead repelled many people; in England and America, dissection was a punishment reserved for executed criminals rather than respectable citizens. For their part, physicians valued anatomical dissection

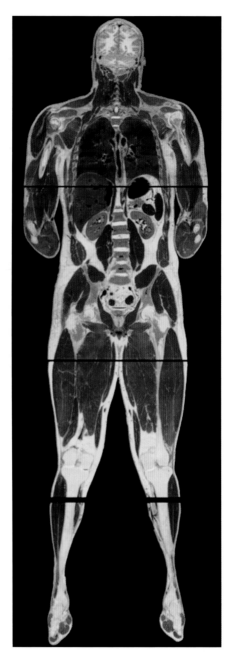

This is an image available over the Internet from the National Library of Medicine's Visible Human Project, the world's first computerized library of human anatomy at www.nlm.nih.gov.

as an essential prerequisite for medical training and the advance of medical knowledge. After decades of campaigning and much public education about the need for autopsy and dissection to advance medical knowledge, as well as the reassurance that bodies of the dead would be treated with respect, the medical profession overcame much of the traditional aversion to dissection. By the early twentieth century most American states passed laws that enabled doctors and researchers to legally obtain unclaimed dead bodies for research and education. Today physicians and medical educators also rely on people who are willing to bequeath their bodies for medical use after their deaths.

In the 1990s revolutionary changes in technology have created unparalleled access to knowledge of human anatomy. Through the use of computer-assisted tomography (CAT), magnetic resonance imaging (MRI), and the Internet, The Visible Human Project, sponsored by the National Library of Medicine, has produced what director Donald A.B. Lindberg, M.D. described as "computerized cadavers." Beginning in 1993, researchers at the University of Colorado used two human cadavers (the bodies of a thirty-nine-year-old man and a fifty-nine-year-old woman) to create computer models of the human body. Unlike Victor Frankenstein who stole body parts from the graveyard, researchers were able to use the body of executed murderer Joseph Paul Jernigan, who gave permission for his body to be used following his death by lethal injection, and the body of a Maryland woman who also bequeathed her body for use in research.[98]

Images from The Visible Human Project, created by electronic imaging and by slicing and photographing thousands of razor-thin tissue sections from the cadavers, are accessible on the Internet through the National Library of Medicine at http://www.nlm.nih.gov. These images have already been used to teach young doctors medical procedures and to train physicians in novel surgical techniques. At the University of Colorado Health Sciences Center, simulator "patients" allow anesthesiology residents to experience electronically the feel of bone and muscles during injections before they administer drugs to real human beings. Information from The Visible Human Project enabled researcher Gary Hack and his team at the University of Maryland Dental School to confirm the discovery of two previously unknown anatomical structures, both a muscle in the jaw and a band of connective tissue between one of the deep neck muscles and the dura (the sheath covering the brain and spinal column). "The Visible Human data set that we used to help confirm this connection [between the muscle and the dura]," explained Hack, "now can help us discover what this connective tissue does, which may be an important piece in the puzzle of head and neck pain."

The Price of Secrecy

The fear that scientific advances incompletely understood or uncontrolled will wreak havoc is a persistent feature of the Frankenstein story in the late twentieth century. Yet Mary Shelley identified another feature of scientific research that many Americans find disturbing today: the idea that scientists, rather than openly sharing their information and the results of their experiments, would keep silent about their research and its implications. In Shelley's novel, one of the most corrosive effects of Victor Frankenstein's pursuit of the principle of life is his failure to act responsibly after the monster begins his murderous rampage. Rather than reveal what he knows about the murder of his young brother William, Frankenstein says nothing. By remaining silent, he allows an innocent girl to be executed for the crime, and he similarly conceals the true nature of the murderer of both his close friend and his wife. It is this culpable failure on the part of Victor Frankenstein, both his abandonment of his creature and his suppression of the truth, that leads to the monster's brutality and the novel's tragic end.

That governments or individual scientists could similarly conduct research in secret and could involve unknowing citizens in their experiments has troubled many Americans in recent years. In 1994 reports in the national press about secret government radiation experiments conducted on unsuspecting American citizens during the Cold War prompted President Bill Clinton to appoint a committee to investigate such charges. In 1995 following the committee's report, the President apologized on behalf of the nation to the men, women, and children who had participated without their knowledge or consent in radiation-related research.[99]

Another example of scientific research conducted in secret or without much public scrutiny before the 1990s is research involving tobacco and nicotine. In

© Stephen Crowley/The New York Times

On April 14, 1994, chairmen of the leading tobacco companies testified before Congress that nicotine is not addictive.

1964 Surgeon General Luther Terry released the now famous report *Smoking and Health*, which concluded that cigarette smoking caused lung cancer in men. The report did not identify tobacco as addictive. At the same time, however, scientists working for the tobacco industries found that nicotine was in fact an addictive drug. By 1963, for example, scientists at the Brown and Williamson Tobacco Corporation conceded that nicotine was physiologically active, addictive, and that cigarettes functioned as "nicotine delivery devices."[100] Such information known to the tobacco industry from its own scientists was withheld from the committee that advised the Surgeon General in making his report. "One can speculate, with enormous regret," observed former Surgeon General C. Everett Koop, "how different the 1964 Surgeon General's report would have been had the tobacco companies shared their research with the Surgeon General's Advisory Committee."[101] One can also speculate about the number of lives that might have been saved by earlier disclosure of the injurious effects of tobacco smoke and nicotine.

Accessibility and openness are essential elements of the Human Genome Project, an international research effort begun in 1990 devoted to identifying all human genes and generating a complete sequence of human DNA. Physicians

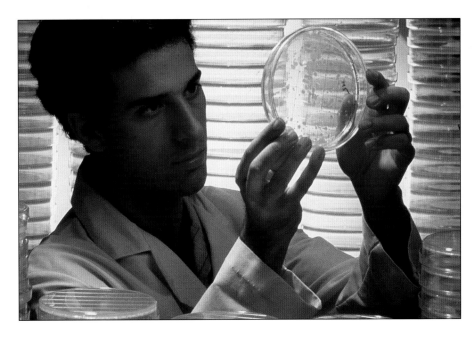

Agar Plates
Photograph by Bill Branson
Courtesy National Cancer Institute

A scientist at the Laboratory of Cellular and Molecular Biology at the National Cancer Institute examines bacteria from which DNA is extracted for further study.

and scientists believe that this information will revolutionize clinical practice and research, and lead to new diagnostic tests for inherited diseases, as well as more effective therapies and preventive measures. In order to encourage further research and to maximize the benefits to society, the National Human Genome Research Institute (NHGRI) of the National Institutes of Health in 1996 adopted a policy that all human genomic DNA sequence data, produced under grants from the NHGRI, be released as quickly as possible. In addition to its quick dissemination, the policy calls for scientists to place the data in the public domain where it can be accessed by other researchers.[102] This insistence on openness and access contrasts sharply with Mary Shelley's scientist who withholds the details of his methods in bringing the creature to life and fails to speak out when his monster begins his murderous rampage.

Cloning report on Cable News Network
©1997 Cable News Network Inc.
All rights reserved.

News programs, talk shows, and made-for-tele-vision movies all helped make cloning a topic of discussion and debate in American living rooms.

Newsweek, March 10, 1997
©1997 Newsweek, Inc. All rights reserved.
Reprinted by permission. Photography courtesy Tom Haynes.

When news that Scottish researcher Ian Wilmut had successfully cloned an adult sheep (named Dolly) reached the public, questions about the human implications of this powerful new technology erupted in many different forms. In magazines, newspapers, television programs, and over the Internet, people debated the future of cloning research. Not surprisingly, given the power of the Frankenstein myth, some interpreted the reports about Dolly in terms of the monster: "The most immediate medical consequences of cloning the Scottish sheep Dolly," noted a contributor to the *Washington Post*, "has been a major outbreak of the Frankenstein syndrome."[103] By this, the writer meant fears about a force of evil unleashed by science on an unsuspecting world.

Cloning, like other stunning scientific advances in the last decade, raises difficult ethical and policy questions. Should scientists proceed without any constraints on their activities? How do we resolve the conflict between the desire to advance scientific knowledge and the fears that such progress will create undesired consequences (a monster, Mary Shelley might say)? How can we negotiate the boundaries of acceptable science and social policy?

In order to address social and ethical concerns about human cloning, President Bill Clinton in February 1997 announced a moratorium on human cloning, and asked the recently established National Bioethics Advisory Commission to investigate the legal, ethical, and scientific implications of this new development, and to report their findings. The Commission, in a report issued in June 1997, recommended that Congress enact legislation to permit scientists to create cloned human embryos for study and research, but not allow such embryos to be implanted into a woman's uterus and developed into cloned human beings.[104] Commission members adopted such a course to address the publicly articulated fears that the method used to create the sheep would also be used to make children who were identical genetic copies of adults.[105]

Part of the information that the Commission used in its deliberations was testimony from the lay public. In a democratic society, members of the public do have opportunities to voice their concerns in a variety of forums. Amid the exten-

Courtesy Mike Theiler/Reuters/Getty Images

At a June 1997 White House ceremony, President Bill Clinton endorsed a National Bioethics Advisory Commission recommendation on cloning. The Commission urged Congressional legislation to permit the cloning of human embryos for research—but not their implantation into a woman's uterus to develop into cloned human beings.

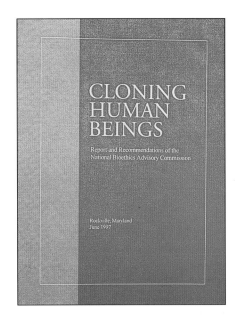

Cloning Human Beings: Report and Recommendations of the National Bioethics Advisory Commission, June 1997

sive media coverage of the cloning breakthrough, a number of individuals expressed their opinions in Internet discussions, in letters to the editors of magazines and newspapers, in interviews with television and print reporters, and at public meetings like those conducted by the National Bioethics Advisory Commission.

Insuring that we as citizens are appropriately informed to confront these issues is an immediate challenge. Unlike Mary Shelley's day where access to medical and scientific knowledge was limited to the wealthy and educated elite, today we have unparalleled access to such information through institutions like the National Library of Medicine, through the popular media, including television, film, radio, magazines, and newspapers, and most recently, through the

"Our sense of ourselves as human beings is very closely linked to our diversity. And the notion of carrying out cloning of the human population, to my mind, is not consistent with the traditional ideas of human individuality and diversity."

Harold E. Varmus, M.D., Director, National Institutes of Health, Congressional testimony, February 26, 1997

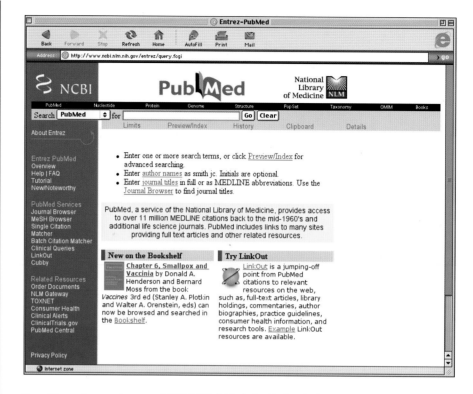

For millions of computer users, MEDLINE/PubMed, the National Library of Medicine's bibliographic database, is just a few clicks of the mouse away—and free. Its 11 million medical citations include more than 124,000 that bear on cloning.

computer-mediated World Wide Web. However, not all sources of information are equally reliable and informative. The challenge, therefore, is how to navigate this ocean of information to educate ourselves about developments like cloning in order to make responsible decisions.

THE MODERN PROMETHEUS

In the subtitle of *Frankenstein*, Mary Shelley invoked the myth of Prometheus. Although Prometheus was punished for his daring in giving fire to his human creations, he remained an optimistic symbol for Mary and Percy Shelley and many

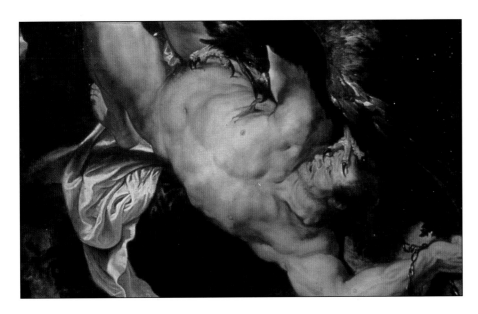

Prometheus Bound, 1611–1612
Peter Paul Rubens (1577–1640)
Photographic reproduction of an oil painting
Courtesy The Granger Collection, New York

of their circle. In the lengthy philosophical poem, *Prometheus Unbound* (1820), Percy Shelley's Prometheus is punished by the gods, but rather than spending eternity in torment, he is eventually liberated by Hercules.[106] When she prepared her husband's poem for publication, Mary Shelley explained that Prometheus "used knowledge as a weapon to defeat evil, by leading mankind, beyond the state wherein they are sinless through ignorance, to that in which they are virtuous through wisdom."[107] Mary Shelley shared this vision. At the end of her novel, as Victor Frankenstein lies dying, he entreats his friend Walton: "Seek happiness in tranquility, and avoid ambition, even if it be only the apparently innocent one of your distinguishing yourself in science and discoveries. Yet why do I say this? I have myself been blasted in these hopes, yet another may succeed."[108]

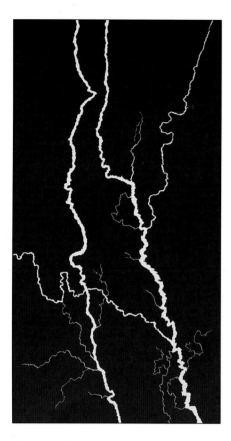

The Blasted Stump, 1984
Barry Moser (b. 1940)
Photographic reproductions of wood engravings from *Frankenstein; or, The Modern Prometheus,* Pennyroyal Press, 1984
Courtesy Barry Moser

NOTES

Curator's Note

In the little more than three years since the National Library of Medicine exhibition, *Frankenstein: Penetrating the Secrets of Nature* opened on October 31, 1997, the Frankenstein metaphor continues to influence and embody contemporary concerns about the biomedical sciences. References to "Frankenfoods" and "Frankenfarms," signaling the potentially monstrous nature of genetically manipulated foods, appear routinely in the popular press. The ongoing controversies involving human cloning, stem cells, and cell lines have similarly fostered reminders of how Mary Shelley's monster shapes the public debates over the uses of medical science. In the past three years, new works on the Frankenstein myth, its origins, and its spheres of influence have contributed to understanding the monster's enduring appeal. In particular, Jon Turney's *Frankenstein's Footsteps: Science, Genetics and Popular Culture* (Yale University Press, 1998), published one year after the National Library of Medicine exhibition opened, offers a valuable exploration of many of the themes pursued in *Frankenstein: Penetrating the Secrets of Nature.*

Birth of *Frankenstein*

1. Shelley, Mary. *Frankenstein*, ed. J. Paul Hunter (New York: W.W. Norton, 1996), p. 172. All references to both the 1818 text and the 1831 introduction come from this edition.

2. Godwin, William. *Caleb Williams*, ed. David McCracken (London: Oxford University Press, 1970).

3. Kelly, Gary. *Revolutionary Feminism: The Mind and Career of Mary Wollstonecraft* (New York: St. Martin's Press, 1992).

4. Lorch, Jennifer. *Mary Wollstonecraft: The Making of A Radical Feminist* (New York: Berg, 1990), pp. 102–103.

5. Clark, John P. *The Philosophical Anarchism of William Godwin* (Princeton: Princeton University Press, 1977), p. 118.

6. Mellor, Anne K. *Mary Shelley: Her Life, Her Fiction, Her Monsters* (Routledge, 1988), pp. 14–22.

7. Mellor, *Mary Shelley*, offers extensive discussion of Shelley's obstetric travails.

8. Moers, Ellen. "Female Gothic: The Monster's Mother," in Shelley, Mary, *Frankenstein* ed. J. Paul Hunter (New York: W.W. Norton, 1996), p. 222.

9. Sunstein, Emily. *Mary Shelley: Romance and Reality* (Boston: Little, Brown, 1989), p. 147. Twenty-eight pounds was the total after the publisher deducted the Shelleys' sizable book bill with the printer.

10. Scott, Walter. "Remarks on Frankenstein, or the Modern Prometheus; a Novel," *Blackwood's Edinburgh Magazine*, II (March 1818): 613–620.

11. [Croker, John] in Shelley, Mary. *Frankenstein* ed. J. Paul Hunter (New York: W.W. Norton, 1996), p. 189.

12. Bennett, Betty T., ed. *The Letters of Mary Wollstonecraft Shelley* (Baltimore: Johns Hopkins University Press, 1980), vol. I, p. 71.

13. "Shelley, Mary Wollstonecraft," *Dictionary of National Biography*, ed. Sidney Lee (New York: MacMillan Co., 1897), vol. 52, p. 29.

14. *The Journals of Mary Shelley 1814–1844*, Feldman, Paula R. and Diana Scott-Kilvert, eds. (Oxford: Clarendon Press, 1987), vol. I, p. 412. Percy Shelley purchased several medical books and encyclopedias, one of which *(Nicholson's British Encyclopedia)* contained a detailed description of how to apply ice in severe uterine hemorrhages. See Nora Crook and Derek Guiton, *Shelley's Venomed Melody* (Cambridge: Cambridge University Press, 1986), p. 241.

15. For Mary Shelley "Beyond Frankenstein," see Fisch, Audrey A., Anne K. Mellor and Esther H. Schor, eds., *The Other Mary Shelley* (New York: Oxford University Press, 1993).

16. Shelley, *Frankenstein*, pp. 171–72.

17. Darwin, Erasmus. *The Temple of Nature; or, The Origin of Society* (Baltimore: John W. Butler and Bonsal and Niles, 1804), "Spontaneous Vitality of Microscopic Animals," p. 5. The philosophical notes are extensive, covering such topics as old age and death, reproduction and sex, hereditary diseases, and Darwin's electromagnetic theory of chemistry. See Desmond King-Hele, *Doctor of Revolution: The Life and Genius of Erasmus Darwin* (London: Faber and Faber, 1977).

18. Farley, John. "The Spontaneous Generation Controversy (1700–1860): The Origin of Parasitic Worms," *Journal of the History of Biology* 5 (1972): 95–125. Farley points out that acceptance of the theory of spontaneous generation waxed and waned during this period.

A Bountiful Harvest for Death, 1779
J.F. Declassan
Photographic reproduction of an illustration from Jacques Gamelin (1739–1803), *Nouveau Recueil d'Osteologie et de Myologie*, 1779

Universal Pictures Classic Movie Monster Frankenstein, 1986
Courtesy Susan E. Lederer
Reproduced courtesy Universal Studios Licensing, Inc.

There Stalked a Multitude of Dreams, 1969
Federico Castellon
Photographic reproduction of a lithograph

Frankenstein wooden push toys
Courtesy Lou Storey

19. Pernick, Martin S. "Back From the Grave: Recurring Controversies over Defining and Diagnosing Death in History," in Richard M. Zaner, ed., *Death: Beyond Whole-Brain Criteria* (Dordrecht and Boston: Kluwer Academic Publishers, 1988), p. 22.

20. Quoted in Jordanova, Ludmilla. "Melancholy Reflection: Constructing an Identity for Unveilers of Nature," in Stephen Bann, ed., *Frankenstein, Creation and Monstrosity* (London: Reaktion Books, 1994), pp. 66–67.

21. *The Journals of Mary Shelley* 1814–1844, vol. I, p. 70.

22. Pelis, Kim. "Blood Clots: the Nineteenth-Century Debate over the Substance and Means of Transfusion in Britain," *Annals of Science* 54 (1997): 331–360.

23. "Transfusion of Blood in Uterine Haemorrhage," *The Lancet* 1 (1834–1835), 157. Pelis, Kim. "Transfusion, with Teeth," in Robert Bud, Bernard Finn, and Helmuth Trischler, eds., *Manifesting Medicine: Bodies and Machines* (Amsterdam: Harwood Academic Publishers, 1999), pp. 1–29.

24. Aldini, Giovanni. *De animali electricitate dissertationes duae* (1794); Pera, Marcello, *The Ambiguous Frog: The Galvani-Volta Controversy on Animal Electricity* (Princeton: Princeton University Press, 1992).

25. Heilbron, J.L. "Volta, Alessandro Giuseppe Antonio Anastasio," in *Dictionary of Scientific Biography* ed. Charles Coulston Gillispie (New York: Charles Scribner's Sons), vol. XIV, pp. 69–82.

26. Schechter, David Charles. "Early Experience with Resuscitation by Means of Electricity," *Surgery* 69 (1971): 360–372.

27. *London Morning Post* 22 (Jan. 1803), quoted in Schechter, "Early Experience with Resuscitation."

28. Mellor, *Mary Shelley*, p. 105.

29. Ure, Andrew. *On Galvanism* (London: Privately printed, 1890).

30. Shelley, *Frankenstein*, p. 32.

31. Marshall, Tim. *Murdering to Dissect: Grave-robbing,* Frankenstein *and the Anatomy Literature* (Manchester: Manchester University Press, 1995) makes much of this connection.

32. Richardson, Ruth. *Death, Dissection and the Destitute* (London: Routledge and Kegan Paul, 1987).

33. Shelley, Mary Wollstonecraft. *Frankenstein; or, the Modern Prometheus*, ed. with introduction by Marilyn Butler (London: William Pickering, 1993), p. xl.

34. Stafford, Barbara Maria. *Body Criticism: Imaging the Unseen in Enlightenment Art and Medicine* (Cambridge: MIT Press, 1993), pp. 256–266.

35. Shelley, *Frankenstein*, p. 34.

36. *The Journals of Mary Shelley 1814–1844*, vol. I, p. 306. The quotation comes from Joseph Forsyth, *Remarks on Antiquities, Arts, and Letters during an Excursion in Italy in the years 1802 and 1803* (1813), p. 34.

37. *The Journals of Mary Shelley 1814–1844*, vol. I, p. 96.

38. Knight, David M. "Davy, Humphry," in *Dictionary of Scientific Biography*, vol. III, pp. 598–604.

39. Davy, Humphry. *Elements of Chemical Philosophy* (Philadelphia, 1812).

40. Ketterer, David. "Frankenstein's 'Conversion' from Natural Magic to Modern Science—and A Shifted (and Converted) Last Draft Insert," *Science-Fiction Studies* 24 (1997): 57–78.

41. Quoted in Smith, Crosbie. "Frankenstein and Natural Magic," in Bann, *Frankenstein, Creation and Monstrosity* (London: Reaktion Books, 1994), pp. 46–47.

The Celluloid Monster

42. James, Louis. "Frankenstein's Monsters in Two Traditions," in Bann, *Frankenstein, Creation and Monstrosity* (London: Reaktion Books 1994), pp. 77–94.

43. Forry, Steven Earl. *Hideous Progenies: Dramatizations of* Frankenstein *from Mary Shelley to the Present* (Philadelphia: University of Pennsylvania Press, 1990), p. 5.

44. Forry, *Hideous Progenies*, p. 11.

45. Baldick, Chris. *In Frankenstein's Shadow: Myth, Monstrosity, and Nineteenth-Century Writing* (Oxford: Clarendon Press, 1987), p. 60.

46. James, "Frankenstein's Monsters in Two Traditions," p. 79.

Frontpiece
Henry Fuseli
Photographic reproduction of the frontpiece from Erasmus Darwin (1731–1802), *The Temple of Nature; or, The Origin of Society*, 1804

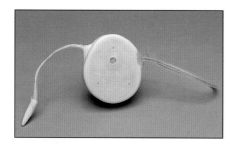

Medtronic Chardack-Greatbatch pacemaker,
ca. 1960
Courtesy The Bakken

In 1932 Albert Hyman described the first external cardiac pacemaker to stabilize the rhythm of the heart. In the 1950s battery-powered implantable pacemakers like this one developed by physician William Chardack and associate Wilson Greatbatch represented a tremendous stride in helping patients with heart disease.

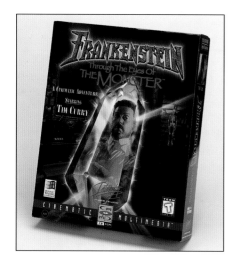

Frankenstein: Through the Eyes of the Monster CD-ROM game
Courtesy Interplay Entertainment Corp.

In the 1990s Frankenstein meets the CD-ROM generation, offering computer users a means to make their own monstrous adventures.

47. Tenniel, John. "The Brummagem Frankenstein," *Punch* 51 (8 Sept. 1866), p. 103.

48. Tenniel, John. "The Irish Frankenstein," *Punch* (20 May 1882), p. 235.

49. Baldick, *In Frankenstein's Shadow*, p. 91.

50. Wheeler, William A. *An Explanatory and Pronouncing Dictionary of the Noted Names of Fiction* (Boston and New York: Houghton, Mifflin and Co., 1878), pp. 138–39.

51. "Frankenstein," *The Edison Kinetogram*, 15 March 1910.

52. Forry, *Hideous Progenies*, p. 80.

53. Forry, *Hideous Progenies*, p. 89.

54. "Frankenstein," *The American Film Institute Catalog of Motion Pictures Produced in the United States, Feature Films, 1931–1940* exec. ed. Patricia King Hanson (Berkeley: University of California Press, 1993), pp. 698–99.

55. *The New York Times Directory of the Film* (New York: Arno Press/Random House, 1971), p. 3.

56. Jones, Stephen. *The Frankenstein Scrapbook: The Complete Movie Guide to the World's Most Famous Monster* (New York: Carol Publishing Group, 1995) offers a decade by decade listing of films featuring the Frankenstein monter and the Frankenstein story.

57. "Frankenstein," *American Film Institute Catalog of Motion Pictures*, pp. 698–99.

58. Gould, Stephen J. "The Monster's Human Nature," in his *Dinosaur in a Haystack: Reflections in Natural History* (New York: Harmony Books, 1995), pp. 53–63.

59. Skal, David J. *The Monster Show: A Cultural History of Horror* (New York: W.W. Norton, 1993), p. 138.

60. *The New York Times Directory of the Film*, pp. 39–40.

61. Gardner, Gerald. *The Censorship Papers: Movie Censorship Letters from the Hays Office, 1934–1968* (New York: Dodd, Mead & Co., 1987), p. 87.

62. "Oh, You Beautiful Monster," *The New York Times* 29 Jan. 1939, IX, 4:1.

63. "Oh, You Beautiful Monster," p. 4.

64. Mank, Gregory William. *It's Alive!: The Classic Cinema Saga of Frankenstein* (San Diego: A.S. Barnes, 1981), p. 26.

65. Skal, *The Monster Show*, p. 132.

66. "1940 Marks Thirteenth Year in 'Age of Mechanical Men,'" Press Release, 15 Sept. 1940, Westinghouse Electric and Manufacturing Company, Pittsburgh, Pennsylvania.

67. Pernick, "Back From the Grave," pp. 52–55.

68. Ford, J.E. "Can Science Raise the Dead?" *Popular Science Monthly* 126, Feb. 1935, 11–13, 108. For an example of press coverage, see "'Dead' Child Kept Alive Six Days," *The New York Times* 25 July 1933, 16.

69. "Fear of Fiend Bars Reviving of Human," *New York Journal* 3 May 1934.

70. "Plan to Revive Dead Told By Doctor," *New York Evening Journal* 19 Oct. 1934. "Medicine: Doctors Have Some Success Making the Dead Live," *Newsweek* 5 May 1934, 3:31. Cornish, Robert E. and H.J. Henriques. *Report of Investigation of Resuscitation* (Berkeley, California, 1933).

71. Gray, Susan M. *Charles Lindbergh and the American Dilemma: The Conflict of Technology and Human Values* (Bowling Green, Ohio: Bowling Green State University Popular Press, 1988), p. 68.

72. Lindbergh, C.A. "An Apparatus for the Culture of Whole Organs," *Journal of Experimental Medicine* 62 (1935): 409–432.

73. "Glass Heart," *Time* 26, 1 July 1935, p. 42.

74. "Artificial Heart 'Revives' Dead Man," *The New York Times* 31 Oct. 1934.

75. "Heart Device Aids Revival of 'Dead,'" *The New York Times* 14 Feb. 1935, 17. For photographs of his pacemaker, see Albert S. Hyman, "Resuscitation of the Stopped Heart by Intracardial Therapy," *Archives of Internal Medicine* 50 (1932): 283–305.

76. Schechter, David Charles. "Background of Clinical Cardiac Electrostimulation," *New York State Journal of Medicine* 72 (1972): p. 612.

THE IRISH FRANKENSTEIN.

The Irish Frankenstein
John Tenniel
Photographic reproduction of an illustration appearing in *Punch*, 1882
Courtesy Pennsylvania State University Libraries

Here John Tenniel depicts Charles Stewart Parnell, a leader of the Irish nationalist movement, as the "Irish Frankenstein." Equating Parnell's efforts on behalf of Irish home rule with the uncontrollable blood lust of the Frankenstein monster, the cartoon was accompanied by text supposedly taken from Mary Shelley's novel.

Electrical Frankie, ca. 1960s
Courtesy Toy Scouts, Inc., Akron, Ohio

77. *"It's Alive!": The Science and Myth of Frankenstein.* Exhibition curator-in-chief: David J. Rhees, Ph.D. Exhibition dates: September 1995–May 1997. The Bakken Library and Museum, Minneapolis, Minnesota.

78. Jeffrey, Kirk. "The Invention and Reinvention of Cardiac Pacing," *Cardiology Clinics* 10 (1992): 561–71.

79. Kevles, Daniel J. *In the Name of Eugenics* (Berkeley: University of California Press, 1985), p. 111.

80. Paul, Diane B. *Controlling Human Heredity* (New Jersey: Humanities Press, 1995), p. 83.

81. Haynes, Roslynn D. "Frankenstein: The Scientist We Love to Hate," *Public Understanding of Science* 4 (1995): 435–444. See also her book *From Faust to Strangelove: Representations of the Scientist in Western Literature* (Baltimore: Johns Hopkins University Press, 1994), pp. 92–103.

82. Tudor, Andrew. *Monsters and Mad Scientists: A Cultural History of the Horror Movie* (Oxford: Basil Blackwell, 1989), pp. 40–41.

83. Skal, *The Monster Show*, p. 132.

84. Glut, Donald F. *The Frankenstein Catalog* (Jefferson, N.C.: McFarland & Co., 1984). This book provides a listing of some 2,666 items, including editions, stories, stage plays, films, cartoons, spoken and musical recordings, sheet music, puppetry, radio and television plays, featuring the Frankenstein monster or descended from the Frankenstein novel.

85. Skal, *The Monster Show*, p. 278.

86. Jones, *The Frankenstein Scrapbook*.

87. Higdon, David L. "Frankenstein as Founding Myth in Gary Larson's *The Far Side*," *Journal of Popular Culture* 28 (1994): 49–60. E.D. Hirsch, Jr. included Frankenstein as an entry in his *A First Dictionary of Cultural Literacy* (Boston: Houghton Mifflin Company, 1989), p. 25.

Peril and Promise

88. Ziolkowski, Theodore. "Science, Frankenstein, and Myth," *Sewanee Review* 89 (1981): 34–56. The author includes such invocations of Frankenstein as that of James B. Conant, who opposed the hydrogen bomb in 1949 on the grounds that "we built one Frankenstein."

89. Hopkins, Donald R. *Princes and Peasants: Smallpox in History* (Chicago: University of Chicago Press, 1983).

90. Miller, Judith, Stephen Engelberg, and William Broad. *Germs: Biological Weapons and America's Secret War* (New York: Simon and Schuster, 2001), pp. 251–53.

91. Allen, Jonathan. "Xenotransplantation at a Crossroads: Prevention versus Progress," *Nature Medicine* 2 (1996): 18–21, on p. 19.

92. Palca, Joseph. "Animal Organs for Human Patients?" *Hastings Center Report* 25 (1995): 4.

93. Malouin, Rebecca. "Surgeon's Quest for Life: The History and Future of Xenotransplantation," *Perspectives in Biology and Medicine* 37 (1994): 416–428.

94. Maugh, Thomas H., II. "AIDS Patient Given Baboon Bone Marrow," *Los Angeles Times* 15 Dec. 1996, section A, p. 3.

95. "Animal Organ Transplants Raise Ethical Concerns," *Science* (18 Nov. 1994): p. 1149.

96. "Americans Recognize Organ Shortage, Support Animal-to-Human Transplants, New Survey Says." 21 January 1998, National Kidney Foundation (http://www.kidney.org/general/news/anim2man.cfm).

97. Institute of Medicine, *Xenotransplantation: Science, Ethics, and Public Policy* (Washington, D.C.: National Academy Press, 1996).

98. "Research Uses Grow for Virtual Cadavers," *The New York Times*, 8 Oct. 1996, Section C, p.1.

99. *The Human Radiation Experiments: Final Report of the President's Advisory Committee* (New York: Oxford University Press, 1996).

100. Slade, John, Lisa Bero, Peter Hanauer, Deborah Barnes, and Stanton Glantz. "Nicotine and Addiction: The Brown and Williamson Documents," *JAMA* 274 (1995): 225–233.

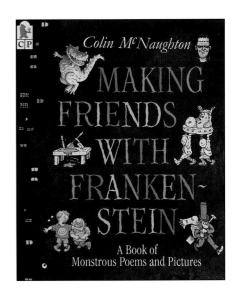

Making Friends with Frankenstein: A Book of Monstrous Poems and Pictures
Colin McNaughton
Cambridge, MA, Candlewick Press, 1994
Courtesy Edwina Smith
Reprinted by permission of Walker Books Ltd., London.

Author Colin McNaughton offers young readers a new slant on "making friends;" in a Frankenstein laboratory complete with body parts in jars and hanging on hooks, a scientist wonders what kind of friend to create for his assistant.

101. Glantz, Stanton, John Slade, Lisa Bero, Peter Hanauer, Deborah E. Barnes, *The Cigarette Papers* (Berkeley: University of California Press, 1996), p. xiv.

102. "Policy on Availability and Patenting of Human Genomic DNA Sequence Produced by NHGRI Pilot Projects" (Funded Under RFA HG-95-005), 9 April 1995, the National Human Genome Research Institute, National Institutes of Health.

103. Trafford, Abigail. "Fear of Cloning and the Ewe To-Do," *Washington Post Health*, 11 Mar. 1997, p. 6.

104. National Bioethics Advisory Commission. *Cloning Human Beings Report and Recommendations of the National Bioethics Advisory Commission* (Rockville, MD, June 1997).

105. Weiss, Rick. "Panel to Back Human Embryo Cloning," *Washington Post*, 4 June 1997, p. A1.

106. Donald H. Reiman and Sharon B. Powers, eds., *Shelley's Poetry and Prose* (New York: W.W. Norton, 1977), pp. 130–36.

107. Grabo, Carl. *Prometheus Unbound: An Interpretation* (New York: Gordian Press, 1968), p. 5.

108. Shelley, *Frankenstein*, p. 152.

EXHIBITION ACKNOWLEDGEMENTS

Frankenstein: Penetrating the Secrets of Nature

The National Library of Medicine wishes to thank David J. Rhees and The Bakken for their collaboration, and the many individuals and institutions who have contributed to this exhibition.

Donald A.B. Lindberg, M.D., Director
National Library of Medicine

PROJECT STAFF

Elizabeth Fee, Ph.D.
National Library of Medicine
Exhibition Director

Patricia Tuohy
National Library of Medicine
Exhibition Program Manager

Susan E. Lederer, Ph.D.
Yale University
Visiting Curator

Abigail Porter
Washington, D.C.
Exhibition Research Coordinator

Edwina Smith
Washington, D.C.
Exhibition Graphics Coordinator

Robert Kanigel
Massachusetts Institute of Technology
Exhibition Scriptwriter

Stephen J. Greenberg, M.S.L.S., Ph.D.
National Library of Medicine
Bibliographic Researcher

Carol Clausen, M.L.S.
National Library of Medicine
Conservation Coordinator

Mary Parke Johnson
Orange, VA
Conservator

Elizabeth Tunis, M.L.S.
Anne Whitaker, M.L.S.
National Library of Medicine
Proofreaders

Nicole Mitchell-Weed
Kensington, MD
Research Assistant

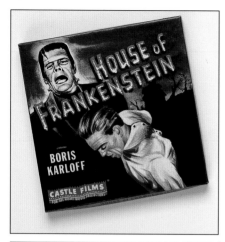

House of Frankenstein (top)
Son of Frankenstein (bottom)
Castle Films, New York
Courtesy Toy Scouts, Inc., Akron, Ohio

DESIGN AND PRODUCTION

Lou Storey
Red Bank, NJ
Exhibition Designer

Troy Hill
National Library of Medicine
Graphic Designer

Gabrielle Pfeiffer
Washington, D.C.
Celluloid Monster, Video Producer

Bill Leonard
National Library of Medicine
Audiovisual Coordinator
The Visible Human—A Step Toward Tomorrow, Video Producer

Exhibits Unlimited, Inc.
Alexandria, VA
Exhibition and Graphics Fabricator

Technical Artistry
New York, NY
Lighting Designer

CONSULTANTS

Mary Fissell, Ph.D.
The Johns Hopkins University

Joe Fitzgerald
National Library of Medicine

John L. Parascandola, Ph.D.
Public Health Service

David J. Rhees, Ph.D.
The Bakken

EXHIBITION DONORS AND LENDERS

The Bakken
Case Western Reserve University
Henry F. Chepulis
Cornell University
Duke University
Bruce Fuchs
Stephen J. Greenberg
Susan E. Lederer
The Harvard Theatre Collection
International Museum of Surgical Science
Interplay Productions
David Kanigel
Library of Congress
Maryland State Anatomy Board
Nicole Mitchell-Weed
Barry Moser
Museum of Science and Industry, Chicago
National Museum of American History, Smithsonian Institution
The New York Public Library
Pennsylvania State University Libraries
Science Museum of Minnesota
Edwina Smith
Lou Storey
Toy Scouts, Inc.
Joan and Kenneth Tuohy
University of Pennsylvania Libraries
University of Illinois at Urbana-Champaign
University of Indiana-Bloomington

EXHIBITION PHOTOGRAPHS AND GRAPHICS

American Philosophical Society

Archive Photos

Ronald V. Borst/Hollywood Movie Posters

Boy Scouts of America

CNN ImageSource

Corbis-Bettmann

Detroit Institute of Arts

The Granger Collection

Tom Haynes

Hearst Corporation

Troy Hill

Library of Congress

Minden Pictures

Barry Moser

Museum of Modern Art, Film Stills Archive

National Cancer Institute

National Park Service, Edison National   Historic Site

National Public Radio

Newsweek, Inc.

The New York Public Library

The New York Times

The New Yorker

Pennsylvania State University Libraries

Photofest

Punch Ltd.

Reuters/Lou Damatteis/Archive Photos

Reuters/Mike Theiler/Archive Photos

Edward Sorel

20th Century-Fox

University of California, San Diego School of Medicine

Harry Ransom Humanities Research Center, University of Texas at Austin

Westinghouse Electric Corporation

CELLULOID MONSTER VIDEO

Columbia Pictures

20th Century-Fox

TriStar Pictures

Universal Studios

THURSDAYS AT THE MOVIES GUEST LECTURERS

Betty Bennett, Ph.D.
The American University

Joseph Bierman, M.D.
Forum for the Psychoanalytic Study of Film

Stephen Hunter
The Washington Post

Patricia E. Gallagher, M.A., M.L.S.
New York Academy of Medicine

Sue Norton
SBN Entertainment

SPECIAL THANKS

Association of American Medical Colleges

Bill Bruegman, Toy Scouts, Inc.

Pat Carson, Special Assistant to the Director, National Library of Medicine

Judy Chelnick, National Museum of American History, Smithsonian Institution

Lois Ann Colaianni

James Deutsch, Film Historian

Classics Illustrated *Frankenstein*
Copyright © First Classics, Inc. 1990
Exclusive License Worldwide.
All rights reserved

Erik Falkensteen, The Granger Collection

Joe Fitzgerald, Graphic Designer, National Library of Medicine

Friends of the National Library of Medicine

Kathleen Gardner Cravedi, Special Expert, Office of Public Information, National Library of Medicine

Alvin Harris, Deputy Chief, Office of Administration, National Library of Medicine

Maryl Hosking, The New York Public Library

Betsy L. Humphreys, Associate Director for Library Operations, National Library of Medicine

Karlton Jackson, Staff Photographer, National Library of Medicine

Ruth Kirschstein, Acting Director, National Institutes of Health

Ramunas A. Kondratas, National Museum of American History, Smithsonian Institution

Ellen Kuhfeld, The Bakken

Laurie McCarrier, McCarrier Graphics

Robert Mehnert, Chief, Office of Public Information, National Library of Medicine

Pamela Meredith

Melanie Modlin, Chief, Publications Management Section, National Library of Medicine

Peggy Parsons, National Gallery of Art

Donald C. Poppke

Elizabeth G. Rosso, Assistant Administrative Officer, National Library of Medicine

Margaret Schlesinger, International Museum of Surgical Science

Candace Schwartz, Designer, Medical Arts and Photography Section, National Institutes of Health

Bruce Sklarew, Forum for the Psychoanalytic Study of Film

Paul Sledzik, National Museum of Health and Medicine

Kent A. Smith, Deputy Director, National Library of Medicine

Tom Stewart, Exhibits Unlimited, Inc.

Michael Stier, Corbis-Bettmann

Ronald S. Wade, Maryland State Anatomy Board

Stephen Wagner, The New York Public Library

Tim F. Wauters, Museum of Science and Industry

Patricia Williams, Administrative Officer, National Library of Medicine

Monique Young

Theodore E. Youwer, Chief, Office of Administration, National Library of Medicine